THE
GOD MODEL

All From One and One From All

By
Phillip Shirvington

The God Model

Copyright 2017 © Phillip Shirvington

ISBN: 9781629671093

Library of Congress Control Number: 2017909447

Table of Contents

Author's Preface

My previous book was a futuristic look at the idea that God is in the process of coming to be, through evolution of intelligence in the universe. However, this idea begs the question: that if there were no God at the beginning, how and why did we get here in the first place? Furthermore, how can one account for the deep devotion to God across the face of the earth if he does not yet exist? While I sought to address this issue in a cursory way with scientific and philosophical speculations, I gave short shrift to the religious argument for a God at the beginning. This essay is an attempt to redress that shortcoming, commencing with a review of the models for God adopted by the many religions of the world, and within them, the different concepts of God held by individuals. Given this great variety, the question arises as to whether a universal God exists beneath the many cloaks he wears? It seems to me that this is so for those with a religious bent; and that this God comes to them through their genes – through human DNA. This book ultimately makes a case for such an idea. In doing so, it is aimed at my fellow man and woman in the street, and not at theologians and philosophers in academia.

Chapter 1

Introduction

When early humans first began to contemplate their own existence, perhaps 100,000 years ago, they no doubt wondered why they were on this earth, whence they had come, what made the sun rise and set each day, and what lay in store for them. In due course, they discovered spirits and later gods who were deemed responsible for these phenomena. About 2,600 years ago the tribes of Israel found a single creator God who knew what they did not, understood what was over their heads, and had power beyond their wildest dreams. What's more, he loved them, his creation. Later, Christians came to believe that this God had a son, Jesus; and, further east, religions with different concepts of god arose. In this way humans replaced a puzzle with an enigma; the unknown with the unknowable. Just who is this God they found? Is there one common thread that runs through the many cloaks that he now wears, and if so, what is it and what is its origin?

The Bible tells us that God made Man after his own image. He then made Woman from the rib of the first man.

This seems to imply that the (traditional) Judeo-Christian God was conceived in male human form, modeled after the biological father. On the other hand, in Islam, which arose out of Judaism and Christianity, another model of God appeared. Although in the Quran God is said to have a face and hands, the traditionalist (Sunni) and the rationalist (Shia) Muslims differ respectively on whether God really has a face and hands, or whether the use of those words in the Quran is figurative for poetic reasons. Both groups do agree that God has speech: it is the Quran. In Islam it is forbidden to portray God in any visual form: it is the calligraphic writing of verses from the Quran in mosques that conveys the presence of God, as God is one with his word.

Whether or not traditional Christians believe in a God as some kind of super human, they seem to mostly agree that God possesses a mind, along with sensory powers and the ability to act on the real world. Since the early Jews and Christians probably believed that we alone among God's creatures possess a mind, then it is perhaps not surprising that many of them should imagine God in some (super) human form. If a cat had a God, he would probably look like a cat.

On the other hand, many modern Jews and Christians, along with traditional Muslims, do not picture God as some wise old man or monarch in the sky. To them, God is a spiritual, indefinable being. We may therefore ask: just where can such a being reside? Is he inside the mind of every human or is he somewhere out in the firmament? Leo Tolstoy, the famous Russian novelist, believed that God is within us all, but Tolstoy was excommunicated for this belief by the Russian Orthodox Church. Like most traditional religions, the Russian Church held that God was external to the human body. If so, we might ask about how such a disembodied mind would work. By analogy, it is now universally agreed by neuroscientists that the human mind, where thought, emotion and memory reside, is some kind of software operating within the electrical circuits of the brain. They can trace activity in the mind to specific locations in the brain. If the human brain is the physical platform for the human mind, what could be the platform for the mind of God out in the firmament? Could it be energizing forces, such as gravity and light, which exist throughout the universe, for example? It is certainly not electrical pulses along neurons in some giant blob of grey matter in the sky, to use an analogy close to our own minds, as such a brain would evaporate in the vacuum of space. Of course, there is a school of thought, espoused by most religions, that God's mind does not rest on a physical platform at all, but exists independently in pure spiritual form.

Perhaps humans cannot expect to be able to comprehend the mind of God, it being so much greater than their own. Presumably, that is why God sent to us prophets such as Moses and Muhammad, and his son, Jesus, in human form, to interpret for us what is in his mind. This is not to mention the scientists he has also sent us, such as Newton, Einstein, Bohr and Darwin, to explain his laws governing the movement of the heavenly bodies and of the sub-atomic particles which make up all matter and energy, and his laws governing the mechanism for evolution of life from primitive single-cell creatures to the complex human being.

Thus said, we cannot help but still be curious about the true nature of God and his mind, since they would seem to have such profound effects on our lives. At the risk of being presumptuous, not to mention sacrilegious, it is the purpose of this book to explore certain models for God that have been proposed over the years, so that we might better understand where he is coming from. Models will be sourced from the Bible and the monotheistic religions and their theologians, as well as from Eastern religions, non-traditional Christians, philosophers, physicists, anthropologists, biologists and psychologists. It is hoped that some common thread running through all religions will emerge from this analysis.

However, it is important not to neglect the individual believer in all this. There are two categories of religion: institutional and individual. Within organized religion, theologians have constructed formal models for God based on logic, philosophy and the scriptures. These models differ, depending on the religious faith, and on the denomination and sect within each faith, of which there are many, especially in Protestantism. However, the individual worshiper, while using the model for God espoused by her religious institution as a template, may have her own concept of God in her prayers and private religious thoughts, depending on her own nature. She may care little for formal models. She may prefer to keep her God an indefinable mystery. She feels the presence of her God privately, and this God becomes a sounding board for all her life choices. She is more interested in how she uses her God than who he is. Many of the devout who report being in the presence of God say that he is beyond description using ordinary language. He is felt rather than seen. Since the personal religious experience of the individual underpins institutional religion (and vice versa), it is important to know the nature and origin of these religious experiences before discussing the models for God provided by the various institutional religions.

To stress the point, we cannot leave the individual out of the picture here, because the human concept of God depends very much on the nature of the believer. If the believer is healthy-minded, then he will have an optimistic view of his life and his God and his relationship with him. On the other hand, if she is a person unhappy with herself and her world, then she will have a pessimistic view of her life, and reach her God through an escape from her sad condition. Her model for God will be quite different to that of the healthy-minded individual.

The reader may question the usefulness of such an exercise to identify various models for God: God either exists or he does not. If he exists then all that is required is faith, as we presumably could not expect to understand a mind many orders of magnitude greater and more complex than our own. If he does not exist, then what is the point of discussing different models for him? Nonetheless, I beseech readers to stay with me on this subject, because even delving into it can throw light on the dark mysteries of the universe, life and the human mind, not to mention God.

The models to be discussed range from the traditional concept of an interventionist, omniscient, omnipresent, omnipotent God, as the creator of the universe and the controller of all our destinies, to the deist God of the

Founding Fathers of America, who was deemed to have set the universe in motion with all its laws, in accordance with his divine purpose, and then let it play out independently of him.

Even within the traditional concept of God there is a range of different types: from the militaristic, angry God sometimes found in the Old Testament and in the writings of Muhammad after he moved to Medina; to the loving, merciful, God as portrayed by Jesus in the New Testament and by Muhammad during his earlier period in Mecca. Interestingly, philosopher Robert Wright claims that these different concepts of God suited the purposes of the faithful at the time. In the time of the Old Testament, the Jews were fighting over land and religion among themselves and with their pagan neighbors, and so a vengeful, angry God was more appropriate. Similarly, in Muhammad's Medina period, the emphasis in his Arab world was on conquest or Jihad, and so a militaristic God was in vogue. On the other hand, the times of Jesus and Muhammad's earlier period in Mecca, when each was concentrating on peacefully winning converts, called for a more loving God.

To add further confusion to the picture is the Christian doctrine of the Trinity in which there is one, and only one, God who exists in three distinct persons: God the Father; God the Son; and God the Holy Spirit. The Trinity was formally stated in the Nicene Creed of AD 325, with the purpose of enjoining all the divine beings mentioned in the Old and New Testaments as the one God. Jews and Muslims do not accept the Trinity.

There is a model for God as the mind behind the universe. Such could be a thinking mind in a God active in the real world, analogous to, but infinitely greater than, our own, consistent with traditional Judeo-Christen theistic beliefs. Alternatively he could be a God of the New Thought religions, such as Christian Science, whose followers believe that only mind exists, and that the material world is an illusion.

On the other hand, God may be a non-thinking form, truth, quality, principle, force or algorithm which moves things along within some inherent pattern, utilizing the laws of physics and choosing the best among the available potentialities for the universe. As we will see later, various parts of this model were proposed by the philosophers Plato and Spinoza, the mathematician Whitehead and the scientist Einstein. Such a God we call nature; and such a belief we call pantheism.

There is an offshoot of pantheism, called transcendental Idealism, espoused by the American philosopher Emerson, a follower of the philosopher Kant. This is the belief that God is "Good" or "Love" or "Peace", and that this God sets the tone and direction for the universe. Stoics, on the other hand, believed that the forces of nature had their own rhyme and rhythm, and the individual might as well become resigned to them good-naturedly. Stoicism was popular in the Greco-Roman world before and after the time of Christ. These offshoots of pantheism tended to enshrine the belief that humankind is one with the divine, that God or nature is all-in-all. Hindus also aspire to be one with God or Brahman, but with the difference that they believe the natural world is an illusion and that only the spiritual world is important. The Sufi sect of Islam also holds this belief.

13

The models presented here range from a God who transcends time to one who acts within time. For indeed, if time commenced with the Big Bang, then nothing could have preceded it, presumably not even God. So if God is put forward as the first cause who created the universe through the Big Bang, then such a God must have been timeless, that is existing outside time. In other words, he created the universe *with* time rather than *in* time. Then we are left with the riddle of how a timeless God can drive events in the real world which exists in time? A related question is whether God is transcendent, that is existing above, other than and distinct from the universe; or is he immanent, and thus always and only present within the universe? Or is he both? For to affirm God's transcendence and to deny his immanence is to arrive at deism. To deny his transcendence and affirm his immanence is to arrive at pantheism.

There is a school of thought that the ultimate endpoint of human evolution is to achieve a level of excellence sufficient to form a union with God. Whether a flawed humanity will ever reach such an exalted state is a debatable point. If it did then this would only be through the triumph of good over evil, of love over hatred and of intelligence over ignorance. Such a model was proposed by Jesuit priest and paleontologist Teilhard de Chardin, with the result that his books were banned by the Catholic Church. However, the Mormon Church and some other newer religions embrace this idea.

Another model for God, not embraced by the monotheistic religions, is that he exists within our own minds. If so, then this implies that God is also present within the structure of living, human DNA, which initiates the development of our brains, and hence minds. Unless, that is, he enters our minds at conception. If indeed God is present within human DNA then why not the DNA of all life forms down to the primitive, single-cell creatures? This implies that God is synonymous with life. Tolstoy, in his novel "War and Peace" exhorts us to love life, even in adversity, because God is life, and to love life is to love God.

Of course, this inquiry would not be complete without examining the hypothesis put forward by many scientists, such as Atheist Richard Dawkins, that the evolution of the universe and life has been just a game of chance played according to the laws of physics; that first life came along with the roll of the dice; and that we humans have evolved from such single-cell creatures through natural selection of the best outcomes out of a series of many lucky accidents during the reproductive cycle over millions of generations. This hypothesis has no need of a God.

A wide variety of models for God will be discussed in the following chapters of this book. However, the aim is to go further: to use this study to point the way towards the existence of a common God beneath the many cloaks donned by him. The threads of this argument will be brought together in the concluding chapter.

Chapter 2

The Nature of Religious Experience

Before moving on to the models for God put forward by organized religions, it is well to discuss the nature of individual religious experience, which both underpins organized religion and is shaped by it. The classic books on this subject are William James's "The Varieties of Religious Experience", first published in 1902 and reprinted over a hundred times since, and "The Individual and His Religion" (1950) by Gordon Allport. A more modern view of the subject, taking advantage of advances in neuroscience, is provided by Malcolm Jeeves and Warren Brown in their book "Neuroscience, Psychology, and Religion" (2009) and by Ralph Wood, Peter Hill and Bernard Spilka in their book "The Psychology of Religion" (2009). Readers are referred to these texts for more detail on the subject than can be covered here.

In recent surveys, 97% of US residents reported that they believe in God, and 90% pray (Gallop & Lindsay 1999).

Churchgoers would undoubtedly affirm a belief in God. Of these 75% report religious experiences (Hood et al). In the US, 79% of the population believe in an afterlife (US GSS 2007). In Europe it ranges from 30% to 60%, except for Ireland and Cyprus which are higher (International Social Survey Program data 1998). In 1949 66% of adults in the US regarded themselves as religious people and at least 90%, by their own report, believed in God (Allport). These levels of religious belief are high despite the modern scientific trend in the West to doubt everything because we do not like to be duped. Although exact statistics are hard to come by in most Muslim countries in the Middle East, one can safely assume that close to 100% of the Muslim citizens would report that they believed in Allah and prayed regularly. The social rewards for doing so can be generous, and the penalties for not doing so can be very severe indeed.

What do all these statistics tell us? That God is everywhere apparent; or that we have been successfully indoctrinated to believe in God; or that we are genetically hard-wired for religion? To answer those questions, we must examine the nature and origin of religious experiences and the reasons people believe in God. William James, a Harvard psychologist and philosopher, was a pioneer in this field. He based his book on a large number of anecdotes from famous and ordinary people who had had religious conversions, hallucinations, feelings of the presence of God, visions and mystical experiences. Most were either religious or had had some religious exposure in their lives. Some of those people had been made saints by the Roman Catholic Church. Among the most important of these experiences are the conversion of Paul on the road to Damascus and the revelations of Muhammad when he wrote the Quran. James got these anecdotes from the Bible, from religious authors, from biographies and from patients and members of the public, who were kind enough to write to him about their experiences. We will come back to James shortly.

Alister Hardy in his 1979 book "The Spiritual Nature of Man" has catalogued a collection of 3,000 religious experiences. The statistical results agree with much of James's anecdotal evidence. Hardy obtained these responses by asking the general public to write in to Oxford University with a description of their religious experiences. Thus this survey did not reveal the percentage of the general public who had such experiences. However, Hardy quotes a 1977 research study by D. Hay of 100 education students in England who were interviewed in depth regarding their answer to the question: "Do you feel that you have ever been aware of or influenced by a presence or a power, whether you call it God or not, which is different from your everyday self?" Sixty-five out of 100 answered "yes" to this question. The more common kinds of experiences recorded by the participants were: awareness of a power controlling or guiding me (23); awareness of the presence of God (22); awareness of a presence in nature (19); and answered prayers (14). Thus some 59% of the "yes" responses could be regarded as religious or potentially religious; the remaining would be better classified as spiritual. By comparison, in a 1985 research study, religious experiences during meditation were only reported by those with a premeditative religious frame (Jan van der Lans, reported by Hood et al, p. 304). This accounted for about 55% of the survey sample. Of the remaining 45%, a good many reported what could be classed as spiritual experiences. One can only speculate as to how many of those spiritual experiences would have been regarded as religious if the respondents had had prior religious exposure. In any event, this research program shows that even in non-religious people, spiritual experiences are recorded during meditation, suggesting that the tendency to have religious/spiritual experiences may be innate in much of the population, and is not solely culturally determined, i.e. does not necessarily require religious indoctrination. Culture only determines the type of experience: i.e. whether religious or not, and in what way religious. More on this later.

Coming back to the work of Hardy, the types of religious experiences reported per 1000 respondents who had religious experiences included: sensory or quasi-sensory experiences (777); extra-sensory perception (245); sense of security (253); sense of joy (212); sense of inspiration (158); sense of enlightenment (195); sense of prayers answered in events (138); sense of presence, not human (201). The experience caused 175 to have a sudden change to a new sense of awareness, conversion or a moment of truth. The initiative for the experience was felt to be: beyond the self, coming out of the blue (124); within the self, but response from beyond, i.e. prayers answered (322). It is worth quoting Hardy's conclusions from his study.

> It seems to me that the main characteristics of man's religious and spiritual experiences are shown in his feelings for a transcendental reality which frequently

manifest themselves in early childhood; a feeling that "Something Other" than the self can actually be sensed; desire to personalize this presence into a deity and to have a private I-Thou relationship with it, communicating through prayer."

Origin

What is the origin of religious experience? Ape-like primates and their human descendants have been evolving for 30 million years. People as we know them have been changing for 15,000 to 200,000 years, and signs of religion, such as evidence of rituals, have existed for 100,000 years. Human ritual goes back to animal behavior, notably mating behavior, which is genetically based. Religious rituals may have hitch-hiked on these ancient traits. Rituals give reassurance in the face of uncertainty. Participation in them is usually voluntary. People enjoy it. It builds group solidarity. It provides a gateway to experiences of trance, often interpreted by the subject as attaining closeness to the spirit world, especially if accompanied by chanting, dancing or marching in step to the beat of a drum, or singing in unison, as described by Nicholas Wade in his 2009 book entitled "The Faith Instinct". Andrew Newberg et al, in their 2001 book entitled "Why God Won't Go Away", claim that ritual turns spiritual stories into spiritual experiences. It converts something believed into something felt, through excitation of the emotions and autonomous nervous system. This something felt is interpreted as proof that the religious beliefs are true.

Religion got its start in pre-historic times. Early humans had been hard-wired by evolution to look for agents in their environment, in human or animal form, as causes for their condition. If no agents could be discerned, spirits were found. There is a long tradition in human history and (inferred) pre-history of belief in mysterious spirits that do not exist within the real world, but have an effect on it. This belief may have arisen more than 50,000 years ago, due to the appearance in dreams of people who were already dead, giving rise to the belief that these dead people were still alive in another world (Wade). Belief in spirits was a pre-scientific explanation for what was often a capricious and hostile world. About 5,000 years ago, in the civilizations living in cities, these spirits were replaced by gods befitting the size and power of such civilizations. Ancient Egypt, Greece and Rome had many gods, which were adopted by the rulers to help legitimize their power. About 2,600 years ago a culture began to emerge in ancient Israel in which only one personal God was worshipped. This God, who was shared among the Jewish community, was the individual's internal source of help when his outside sources, including his own actions, were not enough. Jews, and later Christians, believed that this God made man in his own image. A number of social scientists consider the anthropomorphic tendency to see deities as taking human form and acting and feeling like people to be innate. But this does not explain Asian religions where Gods do not always take human form.

There is a lively debate in academic circles as to whether human religious behavior is genetically or culturally determined. If genetic, then we need to understand how religious behavior could have been naturally-selected. What survivability (adaptive) benefits did it bestow?

Wade suggests that religiosity was naturally selected in hunter-gather societies more than 50,000 years ago through inter-tribal warfare, which was rife in those times, according to anthropological evidence. That religiosity, which in modern days is equated with a desire for peace, should have arisen in the human genome due to warfare is ironic indeed. Notwithstanding, Wade maintains that performance of group rituals in primitive hunter-gatherer societies, which opened the gates to experiences of trances and altered states of consciousness, was believed to enable communication with the spirits who could give protection during warfare. The general excitement and *esprit de corps* aroused by these rituals emboldened the warriors of the tribe ensuring success in the coming warfare and a greater likelihood that the warriors would live long enough to reproduce and pass the religiosity genes along to their offspring. Apparently hunter-gatherers, of which a few were still extant in the 19th C, before being overrun by colonialism, saw no inconsistency between bonding with their own group and enmity towards outside groups who threatened to take their property, their women or their lives. In other words, altruism within the group and war directed outside the group, co-evolved. The in-group altruism was strengthened by fear of punishment for transgressions by the supernatural power that set the tribe's code of behavior (see David Sloan Wilson "Darwin's Cathedral", 2002).

Group natural selection is a controversial theory, as it is contrary to the view of the majority of modern evolutionary biologists that natural selection occurs primarily at the level of the individual; although Darwin himself did suggest group selection as an adjunct to individual selection. The contrary view is that the non-religious individual living within a group may decline to go to war and thus be more likely to survive long enough to pass his genes along to the next generation. However, it is unlikely the group would have tolerated this kind of free-loader, and he would have been drummed out of the tribe, where survival was problematic.

The evolutionary biologist Richard Dawkins claims that religion was adaptive culturally, and not genetically, and passed on to offspring through cultural transmission. He sees this as the most likely route for religiosity to be selected. For example, groups with a common religion may have had survivability benefits through better teamwork. These groups were more likely to survive and pass their culture on to their offspring. However, the widespread adoption of religion among the world's many cultures, often separated from one another by oceans, would be inclined to suggest that the predisposition to be religious, like the facility for language, is innate. Like language it is capable of many different manifestations, which are culturally determined. This innate religiosity/spirituality may well require something from religious culture to set it off.

There have been some attempts to reduce God to a module in the brain, as described by Newberg et al. These ideas have arisen out of the results of brain imaging techniques showing activity in the temporal lobe of subjects who reported religious experiences. This could imply that, during evolution, this God module had been naturally selected as it conferred a survivability advantage, as suggested by Dean Hamer in his 2004 book entitled

"The God Gene". This module should not be seen as being located in one specific spot in the brain, because the brain works in a holistic manner, pulling in help from multiple locations within itself, with its thousands of neuronal cross-connections. This is likely to be particularly so for complex phenomena such as religious experiences, which call on the memory and emotions as well as the cognitive skills located in the temporal lobe. The emotions come from many sources including elsewhere in the cerebral cortex, from the primitive sections of the human brain, such as the hypothalamus and amygdala, and from the hormones, heart and body, which are connected to the brain.

If there is an inherited component of religious behavior, it must have found some way to get into the human mind, which is the brain's operating software where thoughts, memories, emotions and intentions arise. To do this would require an appropriate design of the operating system in the brain. That "software" design, along with the design for the circuits of the brain, must come from human DNA, i.e. the human genome. One's DNA determines the brain's design and development, and how the software of the mind (and to some extent the hardware of the brain as well) is developed in synchronization with the person's unique nature and experiences in the real world, including religious training.

We should be wary of confusing cause with correlation. Just because certain parts of the brain are active during religious experiences, does not necessarily mean that they cause such experiences. It may only mean that the two things happen together, or even the other way around: that religious experiences cause the activity in the brain.

To substantiate this hypothesis that religiosity (spirituality) has been hard-wired into our brains through our genes, it is necessary to show how it got there in the first place. Let us assume that it got there through natural selection (evolution), which was either directed by God, in order to provide a communication channel to him, or occurred under its own steam. If it occurred through evolution then it is necessary to show how religiosity was adaptive. In what way did it enhance the chances of humans who possessed it of living long enough to produce offspring to pass this trait onto future generations? Going back even further, how did religiosity first emerge in our human ancestors over the past 100,000 years? Why did those primitive hunter-gatherers think up the idea of spirits from another world having control of their destinies? After all, this would have been contrary to what their senses were telling them about the real world. As mentioned previously, Nicholas Wade puts forward the idea that early humans started to believe that a life existed beyond death when they had dreams populated by people they knew to be already dead. With this belief in place, it could be argued, for example, that one individual in a certain tribe was born with a chance mutation in his genes. He happened to have been born with a gene enabling him to go into a trance under certain circumstances, during which he had spiritual experiences. According to Newberg et al, this chance mutation could have occurred in the genes controlling the existent neurological machinery governing sexual activity, which creates similar feelings of ecstasy as felt during a trance or a religious experience. Evolution has made sex pleasurable and this is powerfully adaptive for survival of the species. The man with the chance mutation subsequently could have stumbled on his gift by accident. For example, he could have discovered that a trance could be induced by repetitive behavior such as singing, dancing, chanting or drumming or the taking of hallucinogens from certain plants such as mushrooms and cactus. When in such a trance, he (or she) would have experienced feelings of the blurring of the boundaries of the self; of being in a unitary world where there was no distinction between the self, all humanity and the whole cosmos; or of being in an alternate reality. This would have reinforced his belief about the existence of a spirit world, and would have enabled him to convince other members of the tribe of the same thing. It would not have been a big step from this to try to influence the inhabitants of this spirit world to help overcome life's trials, such as poor harvests, winning tribal wars, sickness, etc. A tribe whose members possessed this shared religion would have been much more cohesive and fearless in battle because they would have felt blessed in common by the spirits, and were not afraid of death because they believed in an afterlife to come. Thus, so the story goes, such tribes would have been successful in battle with neighbors, who would have been wiped out, leaving members of the surviving tribe free to produce offspring. That would have included the member who had the trance-experiencing gene, and his blood relatives who may have shared the gene. Through successive generations and successive, successful wars this mechanism would have helped the trance-producing gene to gradually increase in prevalence throughout the population of hunter-gatherers. According to Hamer, there is much anthropological evidence that inter-tribal war was very common among primitive hunter-gatherers of 15,000 to 100,000 years ago.

There are other possible mechanisms which may have naturally-selected religiosity, such as health benefits of religion and economic benefits enabling the group to eliminate free-loaders by insisting on members of the group performing costly rituals. In all cases, in considering whether religiosity was naturally-selected, it is necessary to weigh its postulated positive benefits against the negative ones such as putting one's life in the hands of invisible (and possibly imaginary) spirits, or losing the fear of death. That fear itself is powerfully adaptive in a dangerous and hostile world.

There is much evidence that prayer is good for the health, and mind-cure religions are based on this principle. But it is debatable whether its biological benefit is any greater than transcendental meditation, which is not a religion in the strict sense of the word. Prayer does seem to reduce stress, as it enables the subject to feel she has control over the uncertain. However, it is difficult to see how this could have significantly increased the chances of the individual surviving long enough to produce offspring. Thus it may not have been adaptive during evolution, and thus may be a cultural phenomenon built upon deeper, innate religiosity traits. Forgiveness is also good for the health as it reduces stress, but this is unlikely to have had a genetic component, going back tens of thousands of years, because it has only been a feature of religion since the time of Jesus.

Form

Given that the faculty to have religious experience seems to be innate, by whatever cause, just what forms does it usually take? Psychologists who have written on religion seem agreed that there is no single unique religious emotion, but rather a widely divergent set of experiences that may be focused upon a religious object. James lists these religious emotions that may enter into the religious intention as: religious fear, religious love, religious awe, religious joy and so on. His point is that these generic emotions of fear, love, awe and joy have evolved with us because of their survivability value. They are already in our makeup, and can be appropriated by our religion for its own purpose. Of 500 American students polled in 1949 on the main reason for their religious awakening, 42% said fear or insecurity, 17% sorrow and bereavement, 23% gratitude, and 8% sexual turmoil. In his book, entitled "Religion: its function in Human Life" (1979), K. Dunlap finds that in historical religions, *"interest in divinities generally exists, though not universally. Demons, spirits and souls are commonly but not always a matter of concern. Problems of cosmology and metamorphosis are usually present, but there may be exceptions. Sin, salvation and life after death are topics of only frequent interest. Mystical states, and the idea of holiness are usually, but not invariably included. In dealing with this core of conceptual interests, which is only approximately common, the individual himself experiences an infinite variety of mental states."* Therefore, according to Dunlap, there cannot be just one personal experience of God, but millions of them appropriate to each individual.

To restate the point, the varieties of religious experience not only depend on which of the many religious faiths to which the individual belongs, nor on which of the hundreds of denominations and sects in which he was raised, but also on the inner needs and attitudes of the individual and among different individuals. Therefore the individual's model for God will be almost infinitely variable. Granted, institutional religion achieves some standardization within the one denomination or sect through group prayer, ritual, teaching and singing. This establishes a template from which the individual may model her own private God. But the institution has less control over what the individual does in her own private prayer time and thoughts. Is she the kind of person who is surrendering or self-sufficient, happy or sad, fearful or adventurous, depressed or elated, loved or unloved, guilty or innocent? Her concept of God will be different accordingly.

William James uses a generic definition of religion which allows for this plurality. For him, religion means: "*the feelings, acts and experiences of individual men (and women) in their solitude, so far as they apprehend themselves to stand in relation to whatever they may consider the divine*". Hinduism, for example, admits freely to this plurality of models for God. The Vedas say that "*Truth is One; men call it by many names*". Hindus are given their own private name for God as youths, as their religion recognizes that the temperament, needs and capabilities of the initiate himself must in large part determine his approach to religious truths. An institutional religion has thus recognized the ultimate individuality of the religious sentiment.

There are two parts to religion: institutional and personal. However, every institutional religion has always started with a personal epiphany or revelation in its founder. Generally, if religious feelings, visions, voices from God etc., inspire someone to do better things in his life, then that religious experience can be regarded as real, as it has an effect on the real world. In the cases of Moses, Jesus, Paul and Muhammad, their revelations and inspirations have changed the world and humankind in a fundamental way. What's more these communications from God through the mind of the individual must coincide with electrical impulses in his brain, which neuroscientists tell us, always accompany what is in the mind. Being electrical impulses they are of the physical world, therefore real events in the brain. Yet, these same electrical events occur in the brain of an author while she is writing fiction. However, fiction is not reality; rather it is an extraction from reality, reconstituted. To determine whether a religious experience is real and not a concoction of fiction, we need to look to see if the religious experience has fundamentally changed the life of the subject and others. If it has, then it is different to a fictional event, which usually does not fundamentally change the life of the author (unless her book is a best-seller and makes her rich and famous), or of others. A delusional person will also have electrical events occurring in the brain during a delusional experience. To determine whether a religious experience is real or a delusion, we need to look at the subject's behavior in his non-religious life: if it is rational, then the religious experience is real. In conclusion, if these religious experiences are indeed real, and if God exists in the spiritual world, he must be able to communicate directly with the physical world in the brains of those who feel his presence, perhaps in their sub-conscious state.

Sigmund Freud states that (monotheistic) religion comes from the sub-conscious; that the individual's concept of God is modeled after their physical father. When times get tough, they reach for the father. On the other hand, James speculates that individual mind (consciousness) is part of a universal mind (consciousness). This theory provides a possible channel for the inrush of divine consciousness into the individual mind. It is a common idea in Hinduism, Christian Science and New Thought religions, which we will come to later.

What exactly do we mean by "belief"? Whenever belief receives a great deal of reinforcement, e.g., from the senses, we call it knowledge. Without these supports it is called delusion. In between the extremes, where belief rests on probabilities, as the majority of beliefs do, we speak of faith. In all states of faith, doubt is still theoretically possible, though not actually dominating the mental situation at the moment. Religion thrives in a sea of doubt. The more comprehensive religion becomes, the less comprehensible it is. According to Hood et al, it is precisely this elusive quality of religion and spirituality which makes them so attractive to many people. Wherever there is uncertainty, hope springs eternal.

The shifting ground of religious belief is illustrated in a survey conducted with 414 Harvard undergraduates in 1947, just after the war, of which two thirds were veterans, along with 86 Radcliffe undergraduates (Allport). Of the 200 students brought up in the more traditional Protestant churches, 25% had turned irreligious, 14% claimed that a new type of religion was needed altogether, 19% had shifted their allegiance to more liberal forms of Christianity, such as Unitarianism, or to ethical but non-theological Christianity. We are left with 42% who were content to remain within the tradition in which they were raised. Only 25% of the students believed in the historic pattern of orthodox Christian doctrine. Only 28% of students subscribed to the statement that Christ was the human incarnation of God, preferring to regard him as a prophet. Of the veterans, 55% of them claimed that the war made them neither more nor less religious. Twenty-six percent said that the war made them more religious and only 19% said it made them less so. This shows that different people react in different ways, in terms of their religious beliefs, to dramatic circumstances in their lives.

It is important to distinguish between institutional religion and individual religious experience. Allport makes the point that *"the religious quest of the individual is solitary. Though he is socially interdependent with others in a thousand ways, and requires a religious template from organized religion, yet no one else is able to provide him with the faith he evolves, nor prescribe for him his pact with the cosmos. In the course of its development, the religion of the individual has been refracted by (1) his bodily needs, (2) his temperament and mental capacity, (3) his psychogenic interests and values, (4) his pursuit of rational explanations, and (5) his response to the surrounding culture, especially religious culture".*

Many individuals are attracted to God as a means of handing over the conduct of their life to a superior being, thus achieving an element of control over it. God control is independent of belief in chance, and is good for well-being. There is benefit in having someone powerful in control, and looking after one, providing control over life's vast uncertainties, especially distressing ones, such as death or dying. With respect to death, belief in God makes easy and felicitous what in any case is necessary. Religious ritual and prayer strengthen this feeling of self and God control.

The concept of sin is associated with many religious experiences. The seven deadly sins of Christianity are: gluttony, sloth, greed, lust, envy, anger and pride. Even the absence of self-regulation is regarded as a sin. Sin comes from self-interest and seduction by the temptations of the flesh. Human nature's general tendency towards self-interest has to be counteracted, according to many religions, in order to achieve inner peace. Faith systems encourage congregation into groups to counteract this self-interest. Religions thus build on a basic behavior pattern of humans to act within groups.

There have been many attempts by psychologists to reduce religion to some natural function of the human mind and body. Reductionism in religion was pioneered by Freud. He assumed religion to be false, in the sense that its primary object, God, was not real (in Freud's opinion). In this vein, what a person believes as the reason behind religious behavior, does not matter. It arises from the feeling of being deprived and therefore turning to a belief in life after death to meet current unmet needs. These beliefs are of little importance, according to Freud. So why measure them? On the other hand, William James maintained that the reason why people hold religious beliefs to be true was not an issue. What was important was whether these religious experiences helped the individual or mankind? In the cases of the revelations of famous prophets, such as Moses, Jesus, Paul and Muhammad, they mostly have. James has reduced religious beliefs to their pragmatic value.

What are the supernatural experiences often encountered in a religious context? Usually they are counterintuitive in that they involve happenings or causes that common sense and science would regard as incredible. Supernatural experiences that are counterintuitive may include the following: ghosts; Gods with immaterial bodies; Gods that do not grow old or die; unblocked perception, prescience; statues that "bleed"; statues that hear what you say. Religion is replete with such examples, some regarded as miracles brought on by saints of the Church. Not only religion but also magic and mysticism feature such counterintuitive supernatural experiences.

Both James and Hardy claimed that religious experiences suggest the existence of a transcendent reality, variously experienced. "Transcendent" means "apart from, and not subject to the limitations of the material world". James' evidence was anecdotal; Hardy's was statistical. For example, religious experience can be a resolution of what otherwise might have been a devastating personal defeat – a successful resolution of an inner conflict. It enables the transcendence of previously experienced limits. The resolution of discontent is often the basis of religious experience. Some people achieve this through meditation. However, according to Hardy, the actual practice of meditation elicits a specifically religious experience only for those with a religious frame of reference.

Some philosophers and evolutionary psychologists maintain that religion is an outgrowth of morality, which evolved naturally either genetically or culturally because of its propensity to promote teamwork and community solidarity. James writes that: *"many non-churchgoers claim that they can lead moral lives without religion. But it is not the same. The difference between morality and religion is that morality requires effort and tends to vanish when circumstances deteriorate"* (such as happened during the two world wars). *"On the other hand, religion provides peace of mind even when times are bad. It provides an additional enchantment over and above the feeling of purely moral good. It is solemn and serious. The abandonment of self-responsibility and allowing God to take over seems to be the fundamental act in specifically religious, as distinguished from moral, practice. Christian Science, New Thought, Theosophy and Christianity insist upon it."* Further evidence that morality and religiosity are distinct traits comes from recent experiments with our evolutionary cousins, chimps and monkeys (Wade). A strong code of morality exists among these primates. They have been observed to feel empathy for a member of the clan in trouble, to be aware of a sense of fairness, and to refuse to press a lever that will deliver a tasty snack to them if it causes another member of the clan to simultaneously have pain inflicted upon him. So, morality is innate in chimps and monkeys, and therefore is likely to be so in humans. However, there is no evidence of religiosity/spirituality in chimps and monkeys, so it must have been acquired separately in humans much later in the evolutionary timescale. Many experiments support this contention. For example, humans asked to make moral choices do so at the emotional level, going back to our primate roots, only resorting to reason after the fact. Feeling emotions is innate, although the events which trigger them can be culturally learned. For example, the fear that comes from notice of a tax audit is obviously triggered culturally.

There is also religious happiness and joy. According to James, "*normal happiness has an element of escape in it – escape from hunger, sexual tension, pain, danger, etc., whereas religious happiness has no element of escape in it. A sacrifice is made in the lower world in return for a bonus in the higher world. A higher happiness holds a lower unhappiness in check. Many people regard the happiness that religious belief affords as enough proof of its truth.*"

To understand religious experience it is useful to look at the extremes in its essence, and then tone down. Religious mysticism is one such extreme. For this book, concerned as it is with models for God, it is interesting that an absence of definite sensible images is insisted upon by the mystical authorities in all religions for any successful contemplation of the higher divine truths. For example, the words "soul", "God" and "immortality" have no distinctive sense content whatsoever. The philosopher Emanuel Kant would claim it therefore follows that theoretically speaking they are words devoid of significance, as only things amenable to the senses are objects of knowledge. On the contrary, according to James, "*these ideas have the power to make some people vitally feel presences that they are impotent articulately to describe. Furthermore, records show that when a person experiences the presence of God it can be vivid and far more effective at convincing of its truth than logic can ever be against it. On the other hand, only if logic is combined* with inner feelings and intuition will it succeed in convincing a person to believe in God." Religious mysticism is optimistic and pantheistic. It involves becoming one with God and knowing it. It is embraced by Buddhists, Hindus, Sufis and some Christians. James states that mysticism's *"illusions border on the psychopathic."* It is not intellectual or of the senses. It comes from abolishing the self and feelings of the flesh and descending into nothingness (Nirvana in Buddhism).

Religious conversions, or spiritual transformations, as they are now called, are among the better-documented religious experiences. These usually occur in a social setting provided by the faith to which conversion is made. In conversion or religious regeneration, according to James, *"the change induced in the subject is a transfiguration in the face of nature in her eyes. A new heaven seems to shine on a new earth. The effects of conversion include: loss of worry and anxiety; ability to see new truths. Religious conversions come in two types: slow, like that of Tolstoy, where they have a high intellectual content; or sudden, in the case of St Paul. In slow conversions, the prospective convert is usually drawn into the faith by a sponsor, and his behavior starts to change to fit in with his new social group. After behavior change comes change in personal belief. On the other hand, if a person has a sensitive nature, and has a susceptibility to hypnotic suggestion (i.e. has a passive bent), then he is more likely to have a sudden conversion. Revivalist conversion, which is usually of the sudden variety, always requires the subject to be in great anguish. St Paul's conversion was of the sudden variety, and may have been precipitated by an epileptic fit, to which he was susceptible. Conversion usually brings about a permanent change in one's faith, even if the experience fades."*

Saints created by the Roman Catholic Church usually report prior experiences of God's presence, similar to conversion. Their behavior is changed forever after. The transition from tenseness, self-responsibility and worry to equanimity, receptivity and peace enables the religious martyr to face pain unflinchingly. Yet, according to James, *"in the life of not a few saints of the Catholic Church the spiritual faculties are strong, but there is a deficiency of intellect. This carries the saint to excesses. Devoutness in excess leads to fanaticism in ideologies, the devotion to self and a misguided propensity to praise. An immediate consequence is jealousy for the Deity's honor. This is less a problem when the God is not so intent on his honor and glory, i.e. a less despotic God"*. However, for example, to aggressive characters who are excessively devout, a view of Allah as despotic can lead to fanatical behavior within Islam. On the other hand, in a meek person, this excess in honoring God can be seen as the subject being so overcome by her love that she becomes useless for anything earthly. William James reports this for the Catholic Sister Mary Alacoque. *"She exhibited such paltriness over personal favors won from God, which are not fruits of saintliness worthy of our study. A God dependent on adulation and the granting of personal favors lacks an essential element of largeness; and such sainthood is shallow and unedifying. St Teresa was of this ilk. She wasted her considerable talents in a flirtation with the Deity, which served no useful purpose for humanity."* Yet, she was adored as a saint in former times, and may have strengthened the faith of some of her followers.

Sometimes saintliness goes to excess in purity. According to James, *"the temptations of the flesh, society and materialism are banished from the subject's life so he can concentrate on piety and worship of God usually in a monastery. But, of what use is this sacrifice to humankind?"* That does not mean of course that it is of no use to the individual concerned, who may feel that his life of prayer is for the good of humankind. On the other hand, charity and tenderness are qualities of saints which can never be in excess. They inspire us all to look after those in need.

To summarize, the potential for a significant percentage of humans to report religious experiences of one kind or another, is fertile ground in which the various organized religions can sow their spiritual seeds. Religious experiences only actually occur when the individual already has a religious frame of reference provided by an organized religion. On the other hand, organized religion would soon collapse if adherents did not have religious experiences. These religious experiences are real, firstly because they often change the subject's life in a significant way; and with Moses, Jesus, Paul and Muhammad have changed humankind in a fundamental way. Secondly, these experiences are real because they mirror electrical impulses in the brain, which being physical, are real. The central point, as far as this book is concerned in its search for a common thread running through religious experiences, is that the religious person's God has found a way into her mind in order to impart these experiences. As to how this could come about, we will return to in the concluding chapter. In the meantime, we will now look at how organized religions have provided the frame of reference for individual religious experiences. We will see that organized religions have much in common with respect to community cohesion. They also have much in common with respect to religious practices such as rituals and singing and chanting in unison. This is because these practices lead to religious experiences and hence the religious satisfaction of parishioners. It is with respect to the model for their God and the world in which he dwells where disparities between religions occur, and where there is the greatest call for some unifying thread.

Chapter 3

The Traditional Judeo-Christian God

Parts of this chapter were inspired by relevant sections of Huston Smith's popular book "The World's Religions" (1992) and Jacob Neusner's book "World Religions in America" (2009). Readers are encouraged to consult them for fuller accounts than can be given here.

Judaism

Judaism gave rise to Christianity, the paramount religion of the Western World, and Islam, the religion of 1.5 billion Muslims. How did this come about? *"Israel, in the millennium before Christ, was not the oldest of the ancient civilizations; nor was it among the greatest, that honor going to the Egyptians, Sumerians, Akkadians, Babylonians, Assyrians, Persians, Greeks and Romans. What the Jews brought to civilization was a passion for meaning, particularly in their God Yahweh (or Jehovah). The ancient Jews noted that nothing could be self-created, not even man; he must have been created by something "other" than himself"* (Smith). This, of course, was three millennia before Darwin expounded his theory of evolution of the species by natural selection. *"The ancient Jews further noted that there was an "other" responsible for all the natural events of the world, over which man had no control" (Smith).* Surrounding civilizations in the Middle East had multiple deities responsible for these phenomena, such as a god of storms, a god of harvests, a god of love, a god of war, etc., all of whom were inclined to be capricious and amoral, and indifferent to the plight of humans. *"The genius of the Jews was to see a single, omnipotent God as a combination of all these deities and also being the creator god. What's more this single God loved his creation, especially man, and especially the Jews. The Israelites came to this viewpoint because of God's actions in saving them from captivity in Egypt, as described in Exodus in the Jewish scriptures. They claimed God so revealed himself to them by his actions and his giving of the Torah, including the Ten Commandments, to Moses."* Judaism was a far superior religion to the polytheism practiced in the Middle East and around the Mediterranean at the time, and it was eventually able to displace them all through its offspring religions of Christianity and Islam.

"To make their religion more endearing, the Jews personified God, on the assumption that ultimate reality was more like a person than a thing; more like a mind than like a machine. This followed from the fact that the Jews found greater depth and mystery in people than in any of the other natural wonders around them. Furthermore, if life is to be lived toward fulfillment, there must be a singleness to the personal

God who supports this way. Otherwise confusion would reign" (Smith). Hence the Jews founded monotheism. What's more, in contrast to the gods all around, Yahweh was a moral God of righteousness, compassion and mercy, who was intensely interested in people. Since God created the world, then the world must be good. *"In the beginning God created the heavens and the earth"* (Genesis 1:1) and pronounced it to be *"very good". "Furthermore, an existence that God created, rather than one which arrived by chance, is to confirm its unimpeachable worth, thus giving meaning to the life of the individual"* (Smith).

Judaism (and its offspring) differed from the religions of India and ancient Greece in that it regarded the material world as good, and therefore important, and not an illusion or defective. It differed from (Chinese) Taoism in that God said of the people he intended to create: *"Let them have dominion over all the earth"* (Genesis 1:26). Whereas Taoism required man to live in harmony with nature. *"In Judaism we find an appreciation of nature, blended with confidence in human powers to work with it for the good, which was exceptional at the time"*, and destined to bear fruit in the modern world.

"Jews' search for meaning in their religion is best demonstrated in their interpretation of God's intent in allowing the Babylonians to defeat Israel and exile the Jews to Babylon. The Jewish prophets did not see their God abandoning them, but rather giving the Jews the opportunity to learn from their captivity that freedom was worth having" (Smith).

The Torah has been re-interpreted from its original form by Christians and called "The Old Testament". The God of Judaism is not based on the Christian New Testament, and Jesus is not recognized by Judaism as the son of God, but merely as one of God's latter prophets. Many forms of Judaism do not hold out the prospect of an afterlife; but Christianity and Islam made it central to their faiths.

Christianity

Christianity arose out of Judaism in a series of steps spread over 300 years, beginning with the exemplary life and teachings of a pacifist faith-healer and exorcist in Galilee called Jesus of Nazareth. He soon gathered a band of followers, later disciples, around him, who were overwhelmed by his powers, humanity, humility and egalitarianism. He moved among the poor and the meek and the sick, listening to their problems and healing their maladies. He lived his life as if his ego had completely disappeared under the will of God, whom he was said to have referred to endearingly as "his Father". His followers proclaimed him to be the Messiah who had been prophesied in the Torah to come among the Israelites and free them from the yoke of rule by foreign powers, the latest being the Roman Empire. This claim brought him under the suspicion of the conservative Jewish priests and the Roman authorities. He was accused of treason and crucified on the outskirts of Jerusalem, a huge disappointment to those who thought him the Messiah who would free them from bondage. However, after his body was encrypted, it disappeared, and his disciples claimed he subsequently visited them in Jerusalem and then later in Galilee. Such stories may well have been based on religious experiences of the kind described in the previous chapter. These reports gave rise to the myth (I use this word as there was no historical record of these events) that Jesus had risen from the dead, and therefore he must be immortal and truly the son of God. If he was the son of God then God must have impregnated his mother, Mary. This idea gave rise to the myth of the Immaculate Conception and of his birth in Bethlehem, King David's city, to fit in with the Prophesy in the Torah (Old Testament) that a Messiah would be born there (somewhat inconveniently, Jesus's Mother and earthly Father lived in Nazareth). The disciples set about preaching the story of Jesus all around the Roman Empire, assisted by Paul, who was converted to Christianity when visited by the risen Christ on the road to Damascus (another religious experience). At the same time religious scholars started to put these stories down in written form in what we now know as the Gospels of the New Testament. These contained, inter alia, the reported saying by Jesus that *whomever shall believe in me shall have everlasting life.* Jesus's resurrection was seen as his power over death, and this event enabled the Christians to overcome the fear of death, and to look beyond their miserable existence at the time to a better life to come. The Gospels have much to say about the spirit world. They populated it with angels, cherubs and of course God. It was seen as being distinct from the material world, but existing beside it, and having power over it, examples being Jesus's healing the sick, and Jesus healing the human race.

Although the religion was persecuted and had to remain underground in the succeeding 300 years, it was eventually adopted in the 4th C CE by Emperor Constantine as the official religion of the Roman Empire. In the meantime it had developed a creed, laid down at the Council of Nicaea held in 325 to iron out internal inconsistencies which had crept in over the previous 300 years. One important idea to survive was that God so loved the world that he sacrificed his only begotten son on the cross to atone for the sins of humankind – an idea so compelling that if it were not true it certainly would have been invented. This further strengthened the belief, originally from Judaism, that God loved his people.

Thereafter, religious scholars, such as St Augustine, St Thomas Aquinas and, much later, Cardinal Newman, developed a complex theology. This will be discussed in more detail in later chapters. In 1084, Christianity split into the Western, Roman Catholic and the Eastern Orthodox Churches over doctrinal differences. Later, in the 16th C Protestantism (initially Baptists, Lutherans, Calvinists and Anglicans) split off from the Western Roman Catholic Church, due to disagreements over Church practices.

The idea of the Trinity that God was three persons in one God, the Father, the Son and the Holy Spirit, was formally stated at the conference of bishops at the Council of Nicaea and ratified at the Council of Chalcedon, in order to confirm Jesus's divinity, which was central to Christianity. At the time of the writing of the Gospels, there was nothing startling, as there would be today, in declaring that Jesus, a mortal, was God. In fact many of the Roman Emperors had declared themselves gods to enhance their status. *"It is an important tenet of Christianity that the Incarnation revealed something newsworthy in the Christian message; namely its proclamation of the kind of god that God was, as demonstrated by his willingness to assume a human life of the form that Jesus exemplified"*(Smith). This is central to the Christian model for God.

It will be left to later chapters to describe in some more detail the traditional Christian God. Fuller descriptions can be found in the Bible and the thousands of theological works written since. However, let me just summarize the characteristics of this model for God.

1. He is the creator of the universe and the controller of all our destinies.
2. His son Jesus was born in human form and sent to us to explain what is in his father's mind.
3. God deemed that his son would die as an adult to atone for the original sin, of Adam and Eve eating the forbidden fruit from the tree of knowledge in the Garden of Eden, and for all human sins since.
4. The code of behavior God expects from us is enshrined in the Bible, which is his word.
5. He knows when we have sinned against that code.
6. If we have sinned we are likely to be punished by him in this life or the next.
7. We may seek his forgiveness for our sins through prayer or priest, and this will be granted.
8. If we live by his code and worship him he will love us in return.
9. His love is independent of our station in life, whether we are rich or poor, weak or strong.
10. We may pray to him to relieve our suffering and sickness and that of our loved ones.
11. We may also pray to him to help us win wars and to overcome adversity.

12. If we have obeyed his laws and believe in him, then
    he will grant us everlasting life in heaven, in the
    spirit world.
13. Some believers can get so close to this God through
    prayer that they experience profound religious joy
    or ecstasy.

It is easy to appreciate the tremendous appeal of this God
to the faithful. He gives comfort to their anxieties and relief
to their suffering, whether they are rich or poor. If their life
on earth is wretched, they are offered the prospect of a
better life to come in the next world. While they cannot
all perceive this God with their senses (although many
claim to have done so), they feel he is there and have faith
that it is so. Accordingly, they accept the truth of what is
written in the Bible and what is taught by the Church. In
order to do so, they must suspend their belief in science
and in history, which at times conflict with the words of
the Bible and the Church. It is because of this conflict that
modern Christians and Jews have a different model for
God in which such conflict does not occur.

The traditional Christian's image of God is likely to
be very much a private matter for the individual, but
nevertheless shaped by the model for God offered by
her institutional religion. According to William James, for
many Christians it is more important how they use their
God than in knowing who he is. Furthermore, the typical
Christian may be more interested in what is happening in
her own body and mind, including religious thoughts, than
what is happening in the institutional religion of which
she is a member. Certainly Christians would subscribe as
a minimum to the words of William James that "*religious*

belief consists of the belief that there is an unseen order, and that our supreme good lies in harmoniously adjusting ourselves thereto". This unseen order is what is referred to by Jesus in the Gospels as the Spirit. Christians would go further and believe that this unseen order is overseen by a God who is a person or sentient being; a model which is understandable in terms they are accustomed to as humans. Furthermore, in those terms, no one has come up with a better model or a more convincing explanation for the creation and why we are here on the planet.

"Most practicing Christians may not spend too much time on the theological basis for their God. They are more interested in the poetry of their religion rather than the prose. What is important to them is the prayer, ritual, song, experience and sense of belonging to a community which worships the one God" (Neusner). They are firm in their belief based on their own experience of prayer and the miracle of creation and the works of the countless religious scholars, through the ages, who have written down the scriptures and interpreted them.

Even though traditional Christians worship the one God, the different denominations and sects have different ideas of what their God stands for and what he expects of them. For example, Calvinists believe that God, being all knowing, already knows which humans have been elected to join him in heaven in the next life. This can be a frightening prospect for believers, as they have no way of knowing for sure whether they have been pre-selected to spend the afterlife in heaven or hell. While this theology, which comes from an interpretation of the Bible, is scary, the actual practice in the Calvinist church tends to accept God's graciousness;

and the individual can always rationalize that if she is doing good works and being a devout Christian then that must be because she has already been pre-selected for heaven. Other protestant denominations tend to stress God's graciousness more, and see salvation and heaven open to all practicing Christians.

"Three of the major tenets of Protestantism are the justification by faith, the Protestant Principle, and salvation through the atonement of Jesus Christ for one's sins. The first requires complete faith in God. It is not enough to just do good works. The second involves the avoidance of absolutes, such as saying that a statue is God, or a Pope is infallible, or the Bible is God. This is because the creator God is infinite and cannot be condensed into a book or a mortal" (Smith).

Generally speaking, the protestant religions favor a direct relationship between the individual and her God, one which does not need a priest as a go-between. The Bible is enough of a guide to gain access to God and to lead the kind of life of which he approves. As the Bible is open to multiple interpretations, different individuals and denominations and sects will construct different conceptions of their God, depending on the interpretation they use. This is why there are so many denominations and sects. The more traditional Protestants believe that the Bible is the word of God, and that God, being all-knowing and all-powerful, has made sure that all the translations and theological interpretations of it are true to his word in every detail. This is a tall order when there are multiple translations, versions and interpretations of it. They cannot all be the true words of God, especially if they are in conflict with one another. Lacking a pope who has final authority to decide about doctrines, and depending on a Bible they can interpret in many ways, Protestants will not agree on the details – or even the essentials – of their God.

On the other hand, Roman Catholics tend to relate to their God through the community of the Church, presided over by the Pope as God's representative on earth, along with the retinue of papal officials, monsignors, Jesuits, Dominicans, cardinals and bishops. The Church is the body of Christ, and it is only possible to get close to him within the church through the seven sacraments such as Holy Communion (the Eucharist). By implication the God of Catholics must sanction this approach to him. Catholics tend to see their God through what he has done in the real world. His creations, particularly human life, human marriage and sex within marriage, are seen as holy and therefore fundamentally good. Evil is seen as an aberration. Sin is a mistake which can be forgiven if the sinner seeks reconciliation with God. Men and women can turn over a new leaf, make a new start. If circumstances are dire, they are only temporarily so. All will be well in the end, especially in the afterlife. This is an optimistic interpretation of God.

"The Roman Catholic concept of God differs from the Protestant one partly due to the practice of the Roman Catholic Church of appropriating everything it thought was good, true and beautiful from the pagan religions which it displaced. While this has incorporated experiences from the real world, God's creation, into the religion, it has also introduced concepts now regarded as supernatural" (Neusner). On the other hand, Protestantism went back to the original Bible, especially the New Testament, for guidance about God, this being deemed to be God's word.

To the Catholic, God lurks everywhere in the world, revealing goodness and love. Unlike Protestants, Catholics revere Mary, the mother of Jesus, as a revelation that God is not only the powerful Father to us all, but also has the tender love of a Mother. *"Catholicism has no trouble finding hints of God in such things as devotion to the saints, statues, medals, art and music, even though this is seen by some Protestants as verging on idolatry"* (James). It is in many ways a richer, less austere God than in traditional Protestantism. The Catholic sacramental imagination makes the world a more lovely and reassuring place – perhaps flawed in many important ways, but not inherently evil. Whereas some traditional Protestants tend to see the world as inherently evil and humans as sinners who need God's help to stay on the straight and narrow. More modern Protestants and the new protestant religions, on the other hand, remove sin from the lexicon, and concentrate on the positive aspects of human existence.

According to James, *"Catholic ritual worship appears to the modern transcendentalist (defined in Chapter 5), as well as the ultra-puritan type of mind, as if addressed to a deity of an almost absurdly childish character, taking delight in toy-shop furniture, tapers and tinsel, costumes and mumbling and mummery, and finding his "glory" incomprehensibly enhanced thereby. On the other hand, the formless spaciousness of transcendental pantheism appears quite empty to ritualistic natures, and the gaunt theism of puritan evangelical sects seems intolerably bald and chalky and bleak"*.

The fact that God means many things to different Christians has created schism and even led to bloodshed and executions for heresy within the Christian world, especially during the 15th to the 17th C, when much emphasis was put on identifying the one true God. This is still in evidence today within the more fundamental branches of Islam, where heresy or apostasy can result in beheading. The modern Christian view is that different people and denominations and sects see different sides of the one God. This approach is one of peaceful co-existence, which surely God would wish for among his people.

The traditional Christian God exists in a non-deterministic world, which allows him to intervene if petitioned to do so. On the other hand, some sects believe in pre-destination, that God already knows what is going to happen to them, which implies determinism. A deterministic world is one in which everything has a cause; and the future is fixed or pre-determined, as all its causes already lie in the present, and all the causes of the present lie in the past. Nothing or no one can change this, presumably not even God. Deism (to be discussed in the next chapter) is imbedded in a deterministic world, as God is deemed to have created the universe and the laws of physics, according to his grand design, and then let them be. On the other hand, the traditional Christian God has the power to intervene in the real world, even contrary to the laws of physics. He can do anything he wants. He has also given humans free will to do as they want, and to face the consequences if they make a mistake or commit a sin. This can only be in a non-deterministic world, in which the future is not wholly pre-determined according to cause and effect. That does not mean that cause and effect are not still involved. Without intervention by God or man, they are.

There is a downside to Christian (and Muslim) faith if it becomes blind faith. For example, if the faithful believe everything told to them by a person of the cloth, on the assumption that he is God's messenger on earth, then there is a risk of being seriously misled, as has happened tragically in the past, for example during the crusades and the religious wars in Europe. People of the cloth are mortals, and thus subject to human failings like the rest of us. They can be wrong, and this has led to bad things happening, such as slaughter of non-believers or believers of a different faith or denomination, witch trials, inquisitions with the death penalty for heresy, etc. Nobel laureate for science, Steven Weinberg, is quoted as saying that: *"with or without religion good people can behave well and bad people can do evil; but for good people to do evil – that takes religion"*. To be fair to religion, it must also be said that ideology, propaganda and mass hysteria can also make good people do evil, as was evidenced in Hitler's Germany.

In the United States today, according to Neusner, there are some 900 denominations and sects, although many have recently held joint services. Most churchgoers are Evangelicals, protestants who are interdenominational and maintain that the essence of the gospel consists in the doctrine of salvation by grace through Jesus Christ's atonement; some are Christian Fundamentalists, who believe in the literal translation of the Bible and oppose the teaching of evolution; not a few are Catholics; others are traditional Protestants, such as Lutherans; more than a sprinkling are Mormons, some belong to so-called new-age religions, usually nature-worshipers or Pantheists, or Scientologists, who believe we have led past lives in other bodies; and many are modern Protestants, such as Unitarians or Universalists, whose beliefs are free and diverse, embracing Eastern religions and Western philosophies. For example, such metaphors as "the world is God's body" and "God is mother, lover and friend", rather than "monarch, lord and patriarch" are in vogue in some, especially feminist, quarters. Interestingly, very few Americans (only about 1%) would class themselves as Atheists.

So, even without taking into account individual variation from person to person, the different religious denominations and sects of Christianity may have outdone themselves in the variety of models for God they espouse. We will look at some of these in more detail, starting with Deism, the religion of the Founding Fathers of America. This vast array of models for God will make our task that much more difficult at the end of this book in coming up with a common thread running through all religious models for God.

We can look for commonality using six criteria:

1. Metaphysics. What alternate reality to the material world exists? Is there a spiritual world or a world of mind separate from the material world?
2. Theology. Is there one God or many? Does he dwell in some alternative reality or the material world or both? Is he interventionist or not?
3. Does God provide an afterlife for the believer?
4. What characteristics does this God possess? Is he a person or an indefinable being? Is he angry or

loving or both? Is he optimistic or pessimistic or both?

5. What laws does he promulgate for humans to follow?

6. How do believers communicate with their God? Is it through their minds? Do they have religious experiences during these communications?

In the case of Judaism, 1. A spiritual and material world both exist; 2. One interventionist God exists in one person; 3. God does not provide an afterlife; 4. God is a person. He can be angry and loving, optimistic or pessimistic; 5. God's laws are written into the Torah by divine revelation; 6. Believers communicate with God through prayer or rituals, either privately within their own minds or in a synagogue. Devout Jews pray for many hours of the day, often repeating phrases over and over, accompanied by rhythmic bowing of the head, which may put them into a kind of trance.

In the case of traditional Christianity, 1. A spiritual world and a material world exist side by side. Jesus lived his life as if his ego had completely disappeared under the will of God, exemplifying the extension of the self beyond its boundaries; 2. The one interventionist God exists in three persons. All three dwell in the spiritual world, but God the Son spent some time in the material world in human form; 3. God provides an afterlife; 4. God is generally regarded as a person, but some progressive Christians may regard him as an indefinable being. He can be both angry and loving, optimistic or pessimistic; 5. God requires his people to follow the laws laid down in the revealed Bible, as interpreted by the clergy, to a greater or lesser extent: 6. In the case of Catholics, they communicate with God through prayer, ritual and singing in their church congregation, which through communal bonding extend the self beyond its boundaries. Protestants may communicate through prayer privately or sing and pray in a church congregation. Christians report private religious experiences within their minds.

As we examine other religions and denominations, we will use the above criteria to seek a common thread.

Chapter 4

Deism

Deism arose among the Founding Fathers of America, such as Thomas Jefferson and Thomas Paine, who in turn were inspired and emboldened by writers of the French Enlightenment, including Rousseau and Voltaire, who questioned traditional religion and championed nature and reason. The Founders were also influenced by scientists such as Isaac Newton in England, who earlier had unraveled the mysteries behind the motions of the heavenly bodies. They noted that the heavenly bodies moved the way they did due to the balance between the force which first set them in motion and the force of gravity, and that no God was required to keep them moving in this fashion. While still believing in God, they had to come up with a theology which allowed nature to operate on its own, according to the laws of physics.

In the Middle-Ages, Copernicus and Galileo had shown that the earth circled the sun and so was not the center of the universe as claimed by the Roman Catholic Church; and thus the Church was shown to be fallible. Jefferson and friends were followers of the Protestant, new world, religions, which were less bound by the traditions of the Catholic Church. They sought to come up with a theology that was consistent with science. They knew that everything must have a cause, going back to the birth of the universe and the beginning of time, when there must have been a first cause. Reason told them that since something cannot come from nothing, God must have created the universe in the first place. He was the first cause. At the time, science was not able to explain how the universe began, and so this supposition was not then in conflict with science. Even today, though science has proof of the Big Bang as first cause, it cannot explain beyond a reasonable doubt, how it came about, although there are some compelling theories to this effect, to be discussed in a later chapter.

The framers of Deism thus fixed upon the transcendent model for God; that he existed above, other than, and distinct from the universe; that he was the first cause of the universe, creating it and setting it in motion with its laws, in accordance with his divine purpose, and then letting it play out independently of him. This model adopted the Enlightenment thinking that man had free will, though subject to the laws of nature; and thus God could not interfere with that free will by being active within the world. However, as we will discuss later, it is illogical for man to have free will in the deterministic world which Deism requires.

Although not stated explicitly, the deist God must have created the universe *with* time and not *in* time. For, assuming time began with the birth of the universe, nothing could exist in time before that, presumably not even God. So, the deist God, by definition, must be outside time. He must transcend time. By definition, this God is not immanent: he is not active within the universe. Deism thus rejects the supernatural aspects of religion such as belief in revelation in the Bible, but rather stresses the importance of ethical conduct. Deism is in favor of religious tolerance, hence the freedom of religion enshrined in the American Constitution. It is the belief in God based only on reason and nature.

The Deist differentiates himself from a traditional Christian by applying the test of reason and credibility. The Deist cannot accept that God sent Jesus to earth to die on the cross to atone for the original sin, and all sins since, because this story was invented by Christians many years after the death of Jesus. Likewise, Deists cannot accept the Immaculate Conception, implying that God fathered Jesus, because the only apparent evidence for it is a dream that Joseph had after Mary had come to him already pregnant: that an angel told him to accept Mary into his house as she had been impregnated by the Holy Spirit. Deists do not consider this hard evidence of Jesus's paternity, especially given the (unauthenticated) stories that Mary had been living with a Roman soldier before coming to Joseph. Deists say that only the wonder of creation is hard evidence for the existence of a first cause or God, not the inventions of mortals.

The Deist differentiates herself from an Atheist on the grounds that the evidence for the existence of God is conclusive, based on the wonder of his creation, which we see all around us. Everything must have a cause, and God is the first cause. Everything must have a designer, and God is the designer. Deists are thus creationists; they believe in intelligent design. Accordingly, Deists deny the Atheist's version of events: that the universe, life and human intelligence arose by chance due to a series of lucky accidents over the past 14 billion years. The Deists claim that a clock or computer cannot assemble itself by chance alignment of molecules: It must be assembled according to a design; and a design needs a designer. Thus they claim that nature could not have possibly assembled by chance such a complex entity as the human brain. This criticism of the Atheist's version of events is not completely accurate, as we will see later in this book. Sure, chance would be involved, in the Atheist's view, but it would be assisted by natural selection, which selects the best of the alternatives thrown up by chance, on the basis of their survivability value in the real world.

Deism contributed to the American work ethic: that it is up to the individual to improve his or her own lot in life through hard work, and not to rely on handouts or assistance from God; and that people should not take the defeatist attitude that they are poor because God meant them to be so, in the belief that God would put everything right in the next life. Only a minority of Americans today would call themselves Deists. Deism is an intellectual religion which has little appeal to those seeking a communicative channel and an emotional tie to their God.

A Deist lives in a deterministic world, in which God has chosen not to intervene. Having created the universe, he has chosen to let it play out in accordance with the initial conditions at the Big bang and the laws of physics, in line with his grand design. This grand scheme required evolution of the species through natural selection and survival of the fittest. Out of that process humans acquired a competitive warlike nature towards rivals. This was all necessary for an intelligent species to ultimately emerge. It was part of God's plan, already programmed into the universe and the laws of physics. The next part of his plan would hopefully be for humans to abandon their warlike ways and follow the path of peace.

So, if we apply our six criteria for commonality of models for God to Deism, we come up with the following. 1. In the world in which we live there is only one reality, the material world; 2. At the beginning of time and at the birth of the universe a transcendent God existed to set the ball rolling, and thereafter was non-interventionist; 3. The Deist God does not provide an afterlife; 4. He is an indefinable, distant being, neither angry nor loving, optimistic nor pessimistic; 5. He provides no laws, but allows humans to make their own; 6. He does not communicate with his followers, who are thus denied emotional religious experiences.

Deism has been introduced at this point in the book because it is in a way the most straightforward of the monotheistic religions. It is most rational and most easily reconciled with science and history. By making God transcendent and not immanent and not both, Deism side-steps the logical flaws of having a God who is out of this world and inside it at the same time. Although Deism now has a competitor in science in terms of its explanation of the creation, it does provide a stepping stone for other explanations to be explored in Chapter 15 and the Appendix. What is missing in Deism is the love and emotion infused into a God who lives beside us in our world, as found in the Christian faiths. Not only that, but Deism does not provide a personal channel between a man and his God. A discussion of just how this channel might work is reserved for the final chapter.

Chapter 5

Pantheism, Stoicism, Transcendental Idealism and Buddhism

We diverge from our main topic in this chapter to discuss four movements which are better described as philosophies rather than religions, as in their pure form they put forward no personal God.

We have briefly referred to Pantheism, which is another name for naturalism. It comes in a variety of forms. Spinoza, a pantheist, defined God as: *"that but for which nothing could be or could be conceived to be"*. Since God cannot be separated from his creation, then he is everywhere within it. He is the universe, the laws of nature, life and human life. Einstein believed that nature and the universe were a kind of God. Pantheism has led to a host of nature-worshiping religions, where the sun or the moon or the female fertility goddess or the earth are worshipped. Many of the primitive animistic religions were pantheistic.

Stoicism was a philosophy popular in the Greco-Roman world from the 3rd C BCE to the 1st C CE, the roots of which go back to Plato from an earlier period. Stoics believed in a divine animating principle, called a *Logos*, which permeated the universe and through which all things were made and everything happened. The natural world of the stoics was a deterministic one: humans are all victims of fate and must accept it and face it with equanimity, i.e. with stoicism. Paradoxically, Stoics also believed in human free will for the individual. Stoicism was popular among the rulers of the ancient Roman Empire. Emperor Marcus Aurelius was a Stoic.

The Logos of Stoicism, which means "word" in Greek, was adapted into Jewish theology by Philo of Alexandria in 50 CE, and was later incorporated into the Gospel of John (John 1:1): *"In the beginning was the word, and the word was with God, and the word was God."* The Logos, through which all things were made, was deemed in John to be Jesus incarnate. Thus stoicism and Greek thought, including Plato, had a strong influence on the development of Christianity.

Transcendental Idealism is a philosophy initiated by the followers of Emanuel Kant, such as Ralph Waldo Emerson. Something which is transcendental is presumed in and necessary for all experience. Emerson believed that the universe has a soul, and it is "Good" or "Love"; and our individual souls are part of it. The universe is infused with "Good", and this is what drives it towards good outcomes in the long run. There is no God; only a universal good soul. It is in our power to remove evil from the world; and we will succeed in this. This philosophy took a beating in the aftermath of the horrors of the two world wars in the 20th C. Then it was difficult to find anyone who believed that humankind or the universe was inherently good. Emerson's beliefs were similar to Pantheism, except that they imbued nature with certain (good) values, whereas Pantheism does not.

We will devote a little more space to Buddhism, because it is still very much alive today for many millions of people, especially in the East, and parts of it have been incorporated into some of the modern Protestant beliefs. Much of the inspiration for this section came from relevant chapters of Huston Smith's book "The World's Religions", and readers are encouraged to consult it for a fuller description. Buddhists believe that the world is full of suffering and concentrate on relief of that suffering. Buddhism first took hold in those parts of the world where life was an utter misery. Buddhism was an outgrowth of Hinduism founded in India by Prince Siddhartha Gautama in the 6th C BCE. The founder was disenchanted by the corruption in the Hindu religion, and by the fact that it did not relieve the widespread suffering among the people of India at the time. The lowest castes, whose earthly lives were lacking in hope, had to wait through many reincarnations before being born as a Brahmin, allowing them access to ultimate reality or the God Brahman. Gautama founded Buddhism principally as a right way of life that would reduce suffering for the poor as well as the rich. Since all suffering came from life in the material world, he encouraged his followers to renounce material pleasures, the self, and the ego, and to meditate according to a strict regimen to achieve a state of nothingness, of Nirvana, in which suffering did not exist. *"Nirvana is the extinction of the boundaries of the finite self"* (Smith). Buddhism was founded as a practical philosophy or a way of life, rather than a religion. It originally countenanced no supernatural divinities or gods, nor any religious authority, nor speculated on any cosmology or metaphysics. It held that humans had no soul, even though it accepted that reincarnation occurred in an endless causal cycle of birth and death. *"What was passed on from one life to the next was not an identifiable soul in any substantial spiritual sense, but rather influence through ideas, impressions, feelings and streams of consciousness."* This was claimed to happen in the same way as a candle flame is used to light another: a new flame is born, but it is not the same flame as the first. Buddhists do not believe in the creation, but rather they believe that consciousness and the material world have always existed side by side in an endless cycle of birth, growth, decay and death. To the Buddhist, the material world of phenomena has no intrinsic existence in its own right: it exists only in relationship to human consciousness. The consciousness of a human living today comes not from his brain but from the consciousness of a dead person which has been reincarnated.

The Buddha was reported as being a man of great beauty, with a powerful personality, being highly intelligent and perceptive and a supreme communicator. He wandered India in his early ministry, begging for his food. Adherents were encouraged to follow the eight right ways of living: right views; right intent; right speech; right conduct (including do not kill; do not steal, do not lie, do not be unchaste); right livelihood; right effort; right mindfulness; and right concentration. Buddhism was thus very much a moral code as well as a philosophy of life.

After its founder died, Buddhism took on two main forms: one which remained true to its founder's concept, being a practical philosophy rather than a religion. The other took on religious overtones, invoking the Buddha as a supernatural godhead or divine being to whom supplications and petitions could be made, in a way similar to a personal God in Christianity. The concept of heaven and hell was introduced. Other varieties of Buddhism, which arose after it spread to Central and Eastern Asia, took on various religious characteristics already embedded in the native peoples. "*For example the Tibetan monks engage in a liturgy in which the monks, seated together in long parallel rows, start to chant, beginning with a deep guttural metric monotone which gradually transforms into harmonics that sound like full-throated chords. Throughout the exercise the monks visualize the deities they are invoking (which takes many years of practice) until they are able to see the deities as if they were physically present. In the meditation's climax they seek to merge with the gods they have conjured*" (Smith). This is surely another version of the religious experiences of a God reported by Christians, as described in Chapter 2, and by Islamic Sufis in Chapter 6. These experiences seem to be universal among the religiously inclined, no matter what faith or creed. What's more, as with other religions, Tibetan Buddhist monks have discovered that repetitive rhythmic activity, such as chanting, singing, dancing or drumming, if accompanied by intense meditation to will the self away, leads to a blurring of the boundaries of the self. Meditators in this state may feel that they have entered an alternate reality, into a oneness with all of being, and this can lead to emotional feelings of joy and peace. Newberg et al suggest that these rhythmic, repetitive activities stimulate the quiescent system of the brain, which when pushed to higher levels directly activates the inhibitory effects of the hippocampus, with the eventual result of depriving the orientation area of the brain of neural input, ultimately blurring the edges of the brain's sense of the self. This opens the door to the transcendental unitary states that are the primary goal of religious ritual. The orientation area of the brain is that system of neural connections which tells us what is our body and what is not. Repetitive rhythmic behavior can also affect the emotional state through the limbic system of the brain in the hypothalamus and amygdala, and the autonomous nervous system, connected to them. This can lead to altered states of consciousness, particularly if there is cortical involvement. All these systems in the brain are interconnected with one another, and the effects they produce can be magnified by feedback loops.

One can make the same comment about Buddhism as about Hinduism (to be described in a later chapter): the technique of meditation or concentration, involving a suppression of the bodily functions, especially the mind, in order to achieve the extinction of the boundaries of the finite self, is to shut down much of the cerebral cortex where our thinking and intelligence resides, but also parts of the brain associated with motor actions and the senses. This allows signals to come through from more primitive parts of the brain, associated with the emotions, which are normally swamped by the motor, sensory and cognitive signals. These primitive parts of the brain are within the limbic system, which we share with our animal cousins. It comprises the hypothalamus, the hippocampus and the amygdala, which is in contact with the pituitary gland, the hormones and the sympathetic and parasympathetic nervous systems which give rise to bodily emotions. The limbic system is also in contact with the pre-frontal lobe of the cortex, known to be active during religious experiences (Newberg et al). It could be argued that this technique enables the subject to reach back to an earlier period of his life, or his previous life, or his species, or the universe itself, with which his mind is interdependent, and from which his body arose. This, in order to find insights seated deep in his mind, possibly left there from earlier in human evolution. Buddhists who reach this state claim it enables entry into an alternate reality. The reader must decide for himself whether that world really exists or whether it only exists in the mind of the meditator. While there is much to learn from our uncorrupted minds and our primordial perspectives in order to better understand our present predicament, this is not the direction in which to find the pinnacle of achievements of humanity, which all came along after humans fully evolved their minds and intelligence. Yet for those troubled by the material world, this suppression of the ego and descent into nothingness can be a great refuge from constant suffering.

On the other hand, the claim by Buddhism that nothing substantial, such as a soul, is passed on from one life to the next during reincarnation flies in the face of what we now know of heredity through human DNA. In the first place, the science of heredity does not sit well with the idea of reincarnation per se. Secondly, a child's genetic blueprint comes equally from its biological parents, although it is not exactly the same as any one of them. Thus, while not exactly a soul, a genetic blueprint is passed on from the pool of human DNA through the parents when each child is conceived. Thus the implication in Buddhism that nothing substantial is passed along from previous generations is incorrect.

By the year 1000, Buddhism in India, which 1500 years earlier had broken away from Hinduism, countenancing no gods and no ritual, saw these gradually creep back in. Ultimately, Buddhism in India was absorbed back into Hinduism. In the process, Hinduism took on many of the reforms which Buddhism had introduced.

Christianity is more passionate about the world than stoicism, pantheism, transcendental idealism or Buddhism, which are cold as they do not refer to a personal God, at least in the form in which they were originally founded. To be called a religion, the subject must feel passionate about it, and it should lead to exultation and uplifting. Stoicism, for example, does not do this. It is a form of resignation. Pantheism and Transcendental Idealism are too vague for many people, too lost in the expanse of the cosmos. Rather than a religion, Buddhism, in its original form, is a moral philosophy of life that can provide relief from the troublesome passions of the real world. However, Buddhist meditation has many things in common with a spiritual or religious experience.

If we rate Buddhism according to our six criteria of commonality for a model of God we find the following. 1. There are two realities, the world of consciousness and the material world, of which the first is the most important; 2. There is no God in the formal sense, but meditators often conjure up their own deity or godhead; 3. There is no afterlife, but there is reincarnation in which one's consciousness is inherited from a dead person; 4. There is no God, but the Buddha is held up as leading the ideal kind of life; 5. Buddhists follow the laws of the right path of the Buddha; 6. Buddhists have spiritual experiences during meditation by extinguishing the boundaries of the self, and thereby entering an alternate reality.

As we will see in the coming chapters, Stoicism has achieved a level of influence beyond its ancient beginnings. Its Logos has underpinned Philo's Jewish philosophy and early Christianity. What's more, the Logos provides a basis for a modern teleological view of the universe - an alternative explanation for the creation to that put forward by Christianity, to be discussed in a later chapter. Buddhism is important for this book because it has no personal God in its original form, and thus requires us to widen our net in considering a common thread underlying all religions. But also, by demonstrating the benefits of meditation and deep concentration in taking our minds back to their roots in earlier times, into an altered state of consciousness in which the boundaries of the self are blurred, it gives an important clue as to where to look to discover the deep origin of religious experiences. We have seen some hint of this in Chapter 2. We will have to wait for the concluding chapter to explore this idea in depth.

Chapter 6

The God of Islam

We devote a chapter to Islam, not only because it receives so much attention in the modern world as contributing to the so-called clash of civilizations between Islam and the Western Judeo-Christian faith, but also because it originally arose, according to Islamic history, out of Judeo-Christianity in the deserts of Arabia. It now has almost 1.5 billion adherents throughout the world, and these numbers are growing. The word *Islam* means "peace" and "submission" to God. Many Muslims say "In the name of God the Merciful and Compassionate" each time they begin to speak, read, write, or do just about anything. The word *Muslim* means one who submits to God's will.

Just as Moses in Judaism and Jesus in Christianity hold a special place as messengers and models for their communities, Muslims believe that Muhammad is the revealer of God's will for two reasons. First, he received God's message, which was later written down. This message is the Quran, which is Islam's scripture, like Christianity's Bible and Judaism's Torah. Second, the way Muhammad lived his life is used as an example for believing Muslims today. As we shall see, there are many links between Judaism, Christianity and Islam. By his own admission, Muhammad's message was an attempt to reform the existing religious beliefs and cultural practices of the pre-Islamic Arabia of the 7th C, so as to bring the God of the Jews and Christians to the Arab peoples (Quran 42:13). For example, Moses is mentioned almost 140 times in the Quran. In fact from a Muslim's point of view, it is more correct to speak of the Judeo-Christian-Islamic tradition. Moses demonstrated his prophetic credentials by magic, e.g. turning his staff into a snake and parting the waters of the Red Sea. Jesus did so through miracle healing; Muhammad through God's words and speech, especially through the poetry of the Quran in the original Arabic language. Those seeking a deeper understanding of Islam than can be summarized here should consult Reza Aslan's book "No God but God" (2011) and Huston Smith's book "The Religions of the World" (1991).

Muslims, like Jews and Christians, believe that there is one God whom Muslims call Allah, the Creator, Sustainer and Judge of the universe. In common with the other monotheistic religions, *"Muslims believe that the material world is God's creation, and therefore good. Islam holds that all life is individual: there is no such thing as universal life. The individual soul is eternal. Muslims believe in pre-destination. But humans are allowed free will in matters affecting their own lives within God's overall plan. The Quran uses vivid imagery to describe Heaven and Hell. Most traditional Muslims believe that such places exist. At Judgement Day, it is not enough to have been a good citizen; you must have been also a good*

Muslim. Muslims know where they stand with God: what is forbidden; what is indifferent; and what is obligatory. There is a definiteness in Islam. It is also the most socially explicit of the monotheistic religions. It is very prescriptive. Religion and community are inextricably linked" (Smith).

Although one can know God through the wonders of creation, Muslims believe that God's will was revealed to a long series of prophets or messengers: to Adam, Abraham, Noah, and Moses, then to Jesus, and then to Muhammad, the final prophet. Muhammad claimed that God spoke to him through the angel Gabriel, who told him to recite in the name of and for the Lord who has created man out of a germ-cell. According to Islamic history, Muhammad began to receive a series of revelations through the angel Gabriel, which he recited over 22 years and which became the Quran as the literal and final revelation of God. The Quran was in an almost constant state of flux during Muhammad's ministry, sometimes altering dramatically depending on where and when a particular verse was revealed, whether in Mecca or Medina, whether at the beginning or the end of Muhammad's life. According to Aslan, one scholarly explanation for this is that God could do anything in the manner that he revealed himself to Muhammad, including improving verses. Nonetheless, any attempts by reformist scholars to claim the Quran was meant to address circumstances in Arabia in the 7th C, and not meant to be applicable to modern life, have been met with stiff opposition from traditionalist Sunnis, and in some places the utterers of those words branded as heretics and executed.

Although Muslims believe that God also sent revelations to the Jews through the Torah, and to the Christians in Jesus' message or New Testament, they believe that over time foreign ideas and beliefs corrupted the original revelations to Jews and Christians. Thus the Quran, as revealed to Muhammad, contains the final, uncorrupted, and complete message from God. When performing worship and reciting God's revelation, Muslims believe that they are in the presence of their Lord. Aslan tells us that: *"though in the Quran God is said to have a face and hands, the traditionalist (Sunni) and the rationalist (Shi'ite) Muslims differ respectively on whether God really has a face and hands, though not human, or whether the use of those words in the Quran is figurative for poetic reasons".* So, these represent two models for God within Islam. The God of the mystic Sufi Muslims is a third. The difference between these three branches will be discussed shortly. All three do agree that God has speech, which is the Quran. Although it is forbidden to portray God in any visual form or to have any images of God in any mosque, the calligraphic writing of verses from the Quran on the walls of mosques conveys the presence of God, as God is one with his words. Thus the model for God conceptualized by Muslims is one of an omnipotent, omniscient poet who recites beautiful words: the Quran.

Being a good Muslim has more to do with actions rather than belief. The actions of devout Muslims are enshrined in the Five Pillars of Islam. These are: communal prayer; the paying of alms for the poor, the fast of Ramadan; the Hajj pilgrimage to Mecca; and profession of Faith. The latter is a belief that: "there is no God but God, and Muhammad is God's messenger". This simple message summarizes the Islamic theology, but under the surface lies an exceedingly complex theological doctrine known as the *Tawhid.*

According to Aslan: *"the Tawhid maintains that God is Oneness and is Unity; wholly indivisible, entirely unique, and utterly indefinable. God resembles nothing in either essence or attributes. God is beyond any description, beyond any knowledge. Humans however are allowed to speak of God's attributes in human language, such as "Goodness or "Being", but only with recognition that these are meaningless terms when applied to God. Other attributes include Mercy, Justice, Life, Power, Knowledge, Will and Speech. In all 99 attributes for God are listed in the Quran".*

The faith of every individual Muslim is reinforced by the practice of communal activities (the first four Pillars of Islam). All Muslims, all over the world, look to Mecca and pray five times a day. At least once a week they must pray in a group inside a mosque. Muslims feel part of a world-wide brotherhood. *"Islam is not just a religion, but a communal way of life. By comparison, Christianity is primarily about beliefs, called orthodoxy; and Judaism is principally about one's actions expressed through law, called orthopraxy. Orthodoxy is about myths; orthopraxy is about rituals. Islam started out as orthopraxy as it expanded, but metamorphosed into orthodoxy later due to theological arguments by the religious scholars, called Ulama"* (Aslan).

Unlike Christianity in the Roman Catholic version, Islam does not have a Pope to determine what people are to do or believe. This became the job of the Ulama who devoted their life to study, debate and spelling out as fully as possible God's law. The Ulama were like the great theologians of Christianity and the Rabbis of Judaism in this regard, and they became the teachers and guardians of Islam. Since the Quran and the life of the Prophet did not offer specific answers to every situation, Muslim scholars relied upon their personal interpretations and opinions to determine God's will in a given situation. According to Aslan: *"the view of the Quran as static and unchanging became increasingly problematic as the Revelation gradually became transformed from merely the principle of moral guidance in the Muslim community to the primary source of Islam's sacred law, the Sharia"*. The Sharia was developed by the Ulama as the basis for the judgement of actions in Islam as good or bad, to be rewarded or punished. Because the Quran was silent on many matters of law that arose subsequent to its Revelation, the Uluma had to rely on the *Sunna,* collections of thousands of stories, called *Hadith*, as to how the Prophet lived his life, in order to write the Sharia. This involved tracing these stories, often corrupted with the passage of time, back to their authentic roots. Thus, there was considerable intervention by ordinary mortals in interpreting the holy texts, at least when it came to behavior expected of the faithful. The same holds true for Christianity and Judaism. Since even the Quran and Hadith did not cover every eventuality that arose as time went by, the Ulama had to rely on unanimous consensus of the legal scholars, and other procedures, in order to lay down complete laws for conduct of life and belief. Aslan states that: *"this process transformed itself gradually from trying to be innovative in order to solve emerging social issues to a doctrine of blind acceptance in juridical precedent"*, thus ossifying the doctrine of Islam even more than before. So, we see that despite protestations to the contrary, there has been considerable straying from the words of God in the Quran and the behavior of the Prophet in the Hadith, due to intervention by ordinary mortals, though admittedly endeavoring to be disciplined in the exercise of their discretion. According to Aslan, *"what is obviously the result of human labor, and so plainly subject to changing human biases, can hardly be the infallible, unalterable, inflexible and binding sacred law of God"*. Whereas a Muslim believes he is submitting to God, in practice he is submitting to God's law as interpreted by the Ulama.

Muslims have two main sects: Sunni and Shi'ite, which differ on matters of history, organization and religious doctrine, sometimes bitterly and violently, but they believe in the same God. The majority Sunni trace their history to the Muslim Caliphate, based in Baghdad. The Caliphs succeeded Muhammad as secular leaders of the Muslim world. Their traditionalist beliefs and practices have been described in the preceding paragraphs. The Wahhabi, now based in Saudi Arabia, are the most traditionalist.

The difference between Sunni and Shia is that the Shia believe salvation requires the intercession of Muhammad, his son-in-law Ali, and their descendants (the Imams). This Shi'ite set of beliefs can be summarized as: "There is no God but God; Muhammad is his messenger and Ali is his executor". According to Aslan, *"Muhammad's descendants are the eternal executors of the divine revelation. In the Shi'ite religion, the Imam translates the message of God, and is the only one who can interpret the secret meanings of the Quran, as opposed to the obvious meaning of the words"*. The Imams died out in the 9th C, but a hidden Imam was supposed to have existed in each generation since. The Imam is predicted to return to earth as the Mahdi (Messiah) at the end of time. In the meantime, the Ayatollahs are those who interpret the legal basis of the Shi'ite religion using reason. According to Aslan, the Ayatollah Khomeini in Iran was rumored to be the returning Mahdi in some quarters, but he never claimed to be so. He merely claimed that he was the hidden Imam's representative on earth.

Unlike Christianity, there are far fewer splinter groups and denominations within Islam. This is because the Quran is not only the word of God, but the words *are* God. While there was strong pressure within Islam not to stray from those words, this did happen in two ways. First, as already explained, in the two centuries after Muhammad, the Ulama sought to fill in the gaps where the Quran was silent in order to develop *Sharia* law. Secondly, the rationalists, later the Shi'ites, "*tried to take account of what is rational for God in interpreting the literal words of the Quran*" (Aslan).

According to Aslan: "*by the beginning of the 11*th *C what began as ad hoc gatherings of like-minded Ulama had become crystallized into legal institutions empowered with the binding authority of God's law. The Quran is not responsible for the rigid Sharia law*": it was the historical Ulama who interpreted the Quran to make the law, based on the culture of Arab tribes in the 7th to 11th C, much of which Westerners would now regard as barbaric, particularly that pertaining to the rights of women. On the contrary, according to Aslan, Muhammad believed in equal rights for women, so his ideas have been corrupted by the Ulama.

The modern Sunni world has four main schools of law in different parts of the world. The Shi'ite world has a fifth school of Islamic law. The Ulama associated with these five schools "*entrenched themselves as the sole authority* of acceptable Islamic behavior and the sole interpreters of acceptable Islamic beliefs" (Aslan). In the 20th C the Ulama broadened their audience to play a far more active role in the political developments in their countries, in part through their stewardship of Islam's religious schools or *madrasas*, where generations of young Muslims have been indoctrinated in largely traditionalist beliefs.

In summary, according to Aslan: *"Muhammad's revolutionary message of moral accountability and social egalitarianism metamorphosed into competing ideas of rigid legalism and uncompromising orthodoxy"*. With such a formal, complex and entrenched religious tradition it is very difficult for the Western mind to understand let alone influence Islamic thought.

These days, through the local Ulama, there is some scope for schools to derive their own interpretation of Islam, which unfortunately has sometimes taken an extremist turn. There are two reforming forces in Islam today: the jihadists, really counter-reformers, who want to go back to the traditionalist Islam of the 7-11th C (among them the Sunni Wahhabis) and the modernists who want to reform their religion to make it interface with the modern world. Both are by-passing the established Ulama, whom they regard as outdated old men. The former base their ideology on those interpretations of Muslim scriptures from the Quran, Hadith and Sharia law which favor traditionalism and violent Jihad. Their aim is to re-establish a Sunni Arab Caliphate as a theocracy. The latter are seeking to reform Islam through interpretation of the Quran by alternative Ulama who have sprung up on TV and the internet. The former appeal to a minority of disaffected young Muslim men; the latter appeal to modern, liberal, intellectuals and middle-class Muslims. The former use the sword to persuade; the latter use reason.

So, do Muslims report religious experiences as do practicing Christians? About 75% of Christian churchgoers report having such experiences. Since Muslims and Christians have the same generic human DNA, but differ only in culture, including religious culture, then we might expect the same percentage of devout Muslims to report religious experiences, though in nature they may be different. This is assuming that the faculty for having religious experiences is genetically determined (see Chapter 2 and concluding chapter). The founder of Islam, the prophet Muhammad, had religious experiences for 22 years in the form of revelations of the Quran, *"during which he variously felt something gripping his chest, felt God in his heart, heard the Angel Gabriel, was moved to automatic reciting, heard bells chiming, saw God in his dreams, and ascended to Heaven in a night journey from the Dome of the Rock"* (Aslan). Caliph Umar, the next but one successor to Muhammad, experienced a religious conversion to Islam after hearing the beautiful words of God from the Quran through his sister's window. He was on his way to slay her for becoming a Muslim.

There are one and a half billion Muslims living on the planet. Virtually all pray five times a day, mostly in private. It is difficult to imagine that none of them have religious experiences during prayer; and these experiences would be expected to vary from one person to another, as they do for Christians, depending on the nature, life experience and religious training of the individual. It is also difficult to conceive that the organized Muslim religion would survive for long if the devout had no personal experience of God. Sure, there are important communal reasons for wanting to identify as a Muslim; and in many Muslim countries to be outside the Muslim faith carries penalties, often severe. But we would expect personal belief in God to be the main reason for the Muslim to belong to the faith. Furthermore, it is hard to comprehend that thousands of Muslim Ulama would, through the ages, devote their lives to understanding and interpreting the Quran and Sunna if they did not feel the deep personal presence of God. Finally, though a miscarriage of religion, the fact that suicide bombers are prepared to kill and to die in order to defend what they consider to be the maligned honor of their God signifies that they have had some kind of intense religious experience (no doubt stimulated through indoctrination by the Ulama and the Mullahs).

Before closing this chapter we should discuss the Sufi, the mystical sect of Islam. According to Aslan *"rather than participate in religious communities like other Muslims, they engage in a personal quest for union with God by obliterating the ego, to be utterly drowned in God"*. Smith tells us that *"the Sufis wanted to encounter God now, rather than waiting for the afterlife or for fleeting religious experiences"*. For them, God is the *only* reality, the *only* being with real existence. Sufism is an amalgamation of Christian monasticism, Hindu asceticism, Buddhist thought, Gnostic (non-dogmatic) Islam, and some Shi'ism. According to Aslan, *"for the Sufi, there are many pathways to achieving union with God, none of them important in themselves. What is important is getting there. Sufis believe in an eternal animating spirit, the*

Ruh, which permeates the universe, what the Quran calls the "breath of God". The Ruh is pure being, what the Hindu's call Brahman and Christians call the Holy Spirit". Sufis understand Muhammad as the Gnostic Christians understood Jesus, as the *Logos*, the Greek for "word". "*In the beginning was the word, and the word was with God, and the word was God*" (John 1:1). "*God is to Muhammad like the sun is to the moon, which transmits the sun's reflected light*" (Aslan).

"*To the Sufi, before creation there was only love of God for himself. Humanity is God made manifest; it is God objectified through love*". Sufis do not believe in a dualistic world, of good and evil, the mind and the body. The Sufis are against Islamic law and against the Islamic establishment. They show parallels with a number of other world religions, to be discussed in later chapters. They believe in one ultimate reality, one being, like the Hindu Brahman. Also like the Hindus they believe that the material world is unimportant. Their belief that there is more than one way to God is like that of the Hindus and the Baha'i. According to Smith, "*They believe in obliterating the self, like Buddhists. This involves total abstraction of the self through intense concentration and reaching trance-like states where they can get close to God. In that respect, they believe in a union with God*", like the Mormons. As discussed in Chapter 2, the hunter-gatherers, our ancestors from more than 50,000 years ago, also discovered that they could get close to the spirit world through trances elicited by rhythmic dancing, chanting and singing to the beat of a drum.

If we examine Islam according to the six criteria for commonality in models for God, we get the following. 1. In traditional Islam there are two realities, the material world and the spiritual world. Sufi Muslims recognize only one reality, God in the spiritual world; 2. God lives in the spiritual world, but intervenes in the material world, his creation; 3. God provides an afterlife in heaven; 4. God is an indefinable being, but in human terms is given 99 characteristics, including love and anger. The Sufi Muslims regard him as pure love; 5. Traditional Muslims live their lives according to Sharia law, which was devised by the religious scholars, based on the Quran and the life of Muhammad, with much human interpretation since; 6. Muslims communicate with their God through prayer five times a day. Their founder had religious experiences for 22 years when he received the Quran from God. Traditional Muslims believe in submitting the self completely to the will of God. Sufis drown themselves in God.

Of all religious experiences recorded in all religions, Muhammad's must surely be the most protracted. His contact with God and the Angel Gabriel, as recorded in the Quran and Hadith, give us the best idea of the kind of God he thought he was dealing with. This is the model of God adopted by the Sunni and Shia Muslims. However, it is in the rituals of the mystic Sufi Muslims that we get a present-day glimpse of their God. Like the Buddhists and the Hindus, they resort to meditation, concentration, and entering a trance-like state to experience their God. This gives us another clue that the most intense religious experiences are those when the subject delves deep into the inner mysteries of his mind. This we will take up in later chapters.

We will have more to say about orthodox Islam in the following chapter covering a warlike and angry God

– a God by no means confined to Islam; but in Islam not subject to the reforming and liberalizing forces that have been at work within Christianity over the past 500 years.

Chapter 7

A Warlike, Angry God

In modern times, the characteristics of a warlike God are usually attributed to the God of Islam, who sanctions holy war or Jihad according to some fundamentalist followers. However, holy war and a warlike God are also featured in the Old Testament. So also is an angry God and a vengeful God.

Examples of a warlike God in the Old Testament include God's commands to "*utterly destroy men, women and children*" (Deuteronomy 2:34, 3:6; 1 Samuel 15:3) and statements that Joshua killed "*all that breathed*" (Joshua 10:40). Such passages have been used by Atheists such as Richard Dawkins to claim that the Old Testament God sanctioned genocide and ethnic cleansing. However, biblical scholars point out that these passages should be read as pertaining to a particular time in the history of Israel during which God was fighting for Israel to win back its lands and to expel all those who believed in idolatry, which was contrary to his teaching. Nonetheless these passages may have been used to justify holy war by

Christians over the years, such as during the crusades and the conquests of the Americas by Spain and Portugal.

Examples of an angry, jealous and vengeful God include Nahum 1:2.

"The LORD is a jealous and angry God; the LORD takes vengeance and is filled with wrath. The LORD takes vengeance on his foes and maintains his wrath against his enemies."

Biblical scholars would point out, however, that this passage merely shows God's passion and emotion and his intense interest in the world. The God of the Old Testament desired fellowship and interaction with the other persons in his world; and his anger was seen to be part of the actualization of this desire; or so the story goes. Nonetheless, a reading of parts of the Old Testament can leave the impression that God is a stern father figure who is not averse to losing his temper if annoyed with his children. Inevitably this had the effect of putting "the fear of God" in his flock, which doubtless helped his people stay on the right path.

Philosopher Robert Wright argues that God takes on the characteristics most suited to the times. In the time of the Old Testament Israel was at war with the neighboring kingdoms of Canaan and Moab, whose subjects lived in sin, according to the God of Israel; and they worshipped different gods. God had instructed the Israelites to "worship no other God before me". These sentiments provided the (religious) justification for the Israelites to rid their neighboring lands of people who were sinning against God. They, of course, may have had other more self-interested reasons for doing so.

In Islam there is greater and lesser Jihad or Holy War. The greater Jihad is the internal spiritual struggle of the

Muslim towards submission to Allah – the internal battle between temptations of the flesh and submission to God. The Lesser Jihad is Holy War against non-Muslims based on principle of belief. However, these words, attributed to Muhammad, need to be considered in the light of the circumstances at the time. Muhammad said to his men: *"You have returned from the lesser Jihad to the greater Jihad"* (Aslan). Muhammad used these words as they were returning home after one of his wars, presumably to tell his men that now the war was won they had better get back to being devout Muslims. He may not have been inclined to use these words on the way to war, when his men needed all the inspiration they could get in order to fight.

As is evident from the following quote from the Quran, fundamentalists can find religious justification for teaching and encouraging Holy War: *"Truly Allah loves those who fight in His Cause in battle array, as if they were a solid cemented structure"* (Surah 61:4).

From the Hadith, which records the sayings and deeds of Muhammad, the Prophet said: *"The person who participates in (Holy battles) in Allah's cause and nothing compels him to do so except belief in Allah and his Apostles, will be recompensed by Allah either with a reward or booty (if he survives) or will be admitted to Paradise (if he is killed in the battle as a martyr)._ _ _"* Volume 1, Book 2, Number 35, narrated by Abu Huraira.

Islam's founder Muhammad rarely spoke of war and violence during his earlier period in Mecca when he was concentrating on expanding his ministry and when he was outnumbered by his enemies, the elite of Mecca. However, he did speak in Mecca of retribution against his enemies;

but it was God taking this retribution in the afterlife, not Muslims in the present life. After he moved to Medina, Muhammad frequently used force, or the threat of it, to unify the tribes of the Arabian Peninsula. However, he was also a politician as well as a general and a prophet. He did not give blanket orders to kill all non-believers. He frequently formed alliances with non-Muslims to help him to win wars, and he preached mercy to defeated unbelievers if they were prepared to ally themselves with him and either convert to Islam or pay a tax. The Caliphs, who succeeded Muhammad as leaders of the Arab world, successfully took up arms against the Christian Byzantine Empire in Egypt and the Holy Land, and their Jihad became more extreme than Muhammad's. Islamic Fundamentalists today justify Holy War and the killing of non-Muslims, based on the above passages, and others from the Quran and Hadith. One could say that for the Islamic Fundamentalists, a warlike God sanctions their conquests and terror, as he apparently did for their forefathers.

It is perhaps not surprising that man should envisage a warlike God at critical times in his history. After all, man has it in his own nature to be warlike, having inherited it from evolution; from when his species was fighting against other species and other individuals and tribes of the same species, leading to natural selection through survival of the fittest. Since Israelites and Arabs used their personal God as friend, adviser and confidante, it is perhaps not surprising that they should turn to him in times of crisis, as war surely is, especially if one is under attack. Thus it seems perfectly logical for God to have been given warlike attributes to equip him for such times. Yet surely such a God plants the seeds of man's destruction in these (current) times of huge armies and weapons of mass destruction. Apocalyptic visions aside (to be discussed in a later chapter) there can be no beneficial evolution of humankind from modern war, through survival of the fittest, as the fit, along with the unfit, are likewise annihilated. Thus a God of love, present in the Old Testament and the Quran, but more so in the message of Jesus in the New Testament, surely presents a better way into the future than a God of war. Hence, we may ask whether God sent Jesus to earth with a message to save man from his own nature. As history shows, Jesus has met with only mixed success in this regard. This idea of God sending Jesus among us to bring out our better natures will be explored in later chapters. In the meantime, the next chapter will describe a loving, merciful God.

Chapter 8

A Loving, Merciful God

Whilst the teachings of Jesus as portrayed in the New Testament are the main source in the Bible of a loving, merciful God, there are also many such references in the Old Testament, and in the Quran, especially in those parts of it written during Muhammad's earlier Mecca period.

From the Old Testament:

"The LORD your God is in your midst, a mighty one who will save; he will rejoice over you with gladness; he will quiet you by his love; he will exult over you with loud singing" (Zephaniah 3:17).

And:

"I love those who love me, and those who seek me diligently find me" (Proverbs 8:17).

And:

"Who shows no partiality to princes, nor regards the rich more than the poor, for they are all the work of his hands" (Job 34:19).

And:

"But you, O Lord, are a God merciful and gracious, slow to anger and abounding in steadfast love and faithfulness" (Psalms 86:15).

From the New Testament:

"For God so loved the world, that he gave his only Son, that whoever believes in him should not perish but have eternal life" (John 3:16).

And:

"Beloved, let us love one another, for love is from God, and whoever loves has been born of God. Anyone who does not love does not know God, because God is love" (John 4:7-8).

In Islam, God's love is manifest in his creation. A popular Persian poem goes thus:

"I have not created the creation to get some benefits, I have created people to show my generosity."

God's love for the world in general, and for human beings in particular, is unanimously believed by all Muslims. Indeed one of God's names is *al-Wadud*: He who loves. Every chapter in the Quran except one begins with the phrase: "*In the name of God, the all-compassionate, the all-merciful*". It is noteworthy that although one of the things attributed to God in Islam is the wrath, its application is much more limited compared to his mercifulness and love for his creatures. Indeed, his wrath is only for those who commit evil actions or deliberately disbelieve (tough on those who believe in another God or follow another faith). Muslims regard God's wrath and anger as originating out of his love and mercy, like a father's anger over the transgressions of the son he loves.

Love and for that matter anger and wrath are emotions. If God is deemed to possess these emotions, then he must possess the equivalent of the human body, as well as the brain, in the spirit world. For, in humans, emotion comes not only from the brain, but also from the body, specifically from the effect of hormones secreted into the bloodstream on such vital organs as the heart. For God to be emotional, he must have a body as well as a mind. Believers have no difficulty making this leap of faith. For those who lived prior to the 19th C there was no such leap, for science had by then not traced the human mind to the brain and the human emotions to the hormones in the body. Rather, these were considered to be non-material. In this modern age of science, the leap is more difficult, but concepts of God may also be more fluid.

Now we come to one of the major conundrums for the traditional Judeo-Christian God. If he is all-knowing, all-powerful and all-loving, why does he allow evil and misfortune to harm his flock? The answer goes thus: God has given humans free will. If they get into trouble it is their own fault. In a non-deterministic world, bad things can also happen by chance. God has chosen to let them happen. Some things that happen may seem bad at the time, but they fit into God's overall plan, to which we are not privy. However, no worries, as all will be put right for the sufferers in the afterlife. God knows that there is evil in the world, and misfortune. That is why there is an afterlife for the faithful in heaven, free of such scourges. God is open to letting bad things happen in the material world, such as the carnage in the two world wars, as they are the result of either: chance, which he has chosen not to intervene with regard to; or of bad morals and ungodliness, which need to be punished. That is of course no solace to the innocent in war and the invaded. It does seem though that God does allow good to win out in the end, though only after mass slaughter.

Traditional Christianity has invented the devil as the person who seduces humans into evil. This lets humans off the hook, not to mention God. All evil can be blamed on the devil. Humans can seek forgiveness of their sins if the devil has so seduced them. But, if God is all-powerful, why cannot he overcome the devil in the first place? St Augustine, in the 4th C, argued that God judged it better to bring good out of evil than not to permit any evil to exist. While this is an improvement on invoking a devil, is it rationalization rather than logic?

God's love is a powerful source of reassurance to his people. For to be loved by someone who is omnipotent is to lose one's fear of death, one's guilt and one's dissatisfaction with the self. For God will look after his people in the afterlife. As raised in Chapter 2, putting one's trust in God, surrendering control over one's life to a loving super being, can have a huge calming influence on the individual, particularly if troubled. In a broader sense, if God's love for the individual can be transferred to the individual's love for his fellow man, then there are real prospects for overcoming the warlike characteristics man inherited from evolution. Evolution has placed love deep in the human heart: it just has to be teased out to overcome the tendency to hatred and violence towards outsiders that humans also inherited.

Chapter 9

God as Mind

There is a model for God as the mind behind the universe. Such could be a thinking mind, analogous to, but infinitely greater than, our own, consistent with traditional Judeo-Christian theistic beliefs. An extreme version of this concept is one in which the real world is an illusion, and only mind exists; and mind is God.

One important qualification needs to be made at the outset: if we are considering God as only a thinking mind, then we fall short of the theistic God, who has emotions as well as thoughts. While emotions to some extent originate in the mind, this is not the whole story. In us mortals, for example, the body also has a role. Thus, when I use the word mind in this chapter, I am also including emoting as well as thinking.

The traditional theistic concept of a thinking, compassionate God, places this God in the spirit world. As such, he is beyond the reach of scientific enquiry. He either exists or he does not. If he does, the main evidence for it lies in the record of conversations with God or his angels experienced by the prophets, Jesus and certain chosen people. This record has been written down by mortals, claiming to have had special access to God, or knowing someone who has. We need to be sure that these scribes are not like other mortals in being prone at times to exaggeration, misunderstanding, inaccuracy, imagination, manipulation and ignorance. But how can we be so? Inevitably, we must either accept the holy books, as millions before us have done, believing that God has watched over their translations, revisions and interpretations to ensure they do not depart from his word, or look for evidence of a thinking, emotional God elsewhere, such as through religious experiences. The Deists, on the other hand, have come to the conclusion that the only hard evidence is the wonder of God's creation itself.

As an aside, if, for the sake of argument, we were to presume that we can conceptualize a thinking, emotional God through science, then what are the possibilities? He could be a super intelligence somewhere in outer space, beyond the reach of our radio-telescopes, that is millions of light years away. In which case he would have trouble communicating with us in real time even at the speed of light; and thus we would never know, one way or the other, if he were really there. He could be a mind based on the energy of light (and of dark) and the force of gravity within the universe. Yet, we know of no way that this could happen. He may be in a parallel universe. If so, then we may never know, as science has only postulated parallel universes, and has no hard evidence for them. He could be in another dimension beyond the three space dimensions and time. If so, we may never know, as science has no hard evidence for an extra dimension, and only speculates about the possibility of one. None of these approaches are going to get us very far. We have to concede that the only minds and emotions we know of for sure, from an observational and scientific point of view, are those in humans and the higher animals.

Theologians have proposed various proofs for the existence of a theistic, thinking God, but a close inspection of them exposes all sorts of logical flaws. Some are merely word games disguised as logic. Others argue that the existence of God is the only explanation for phenomena for which science can now provide an alternative explanation. It is impossible to prove that God exists; it is also impossible to prove that he does not. Thus, we are left with the evidence of creation, faith, personal encounters and the word of the Bible as the basis on which to accept that such a thinking emotional God exists. For many that is enough.

There is a school of philosophy, encapsulated in the beliefs held by Christian Scientists, which holds that only mind exists and that the material world is an illusion (see Jacob Neusner's book "The Religions of America" 2009). Everything we think is real is happening only in our mind, which is not dependent on our brain, but is part of a larger mind, which is called God. This idea has lost traction in the general community (but not in some sectors) in recent times, as evidence piles up from neuroscience about the critical role of our material brain in supporting our mind. However, there is a related modern view that we are all in a computer simulation being run in virtual reality by God or some super intelligence, and that whatever we observe and whatever happens in our lives is an illusion. That is, all the motions of the heavens, the laws of physics and the myriad of life forms, not to mention our own feelings, have been programmed into this computer simulation. If we were inside a simulation, we would not know it. We would think our life real. Also, if we were inside a simulation, we would not be able to perceive the person running it. So how are we to know whether we are in one or not? Well, our intuition tells us that we are not, but can we trust intuition?

The idea that the mental world is the only reality and that the material world is an illusion comes originally from Hinduism (to be discussed in the next chapter). It was subsequently adopted in part by Buddhism and much later by Christian Science and then, in more moderate form, by the New Thought Religions originating in the United States. In the case of the latter two, this belief has led to the phenomenon of mental or faith healing. The belief is that God is Mind, and we are part of that Mind. Since Mind is in control, we should appeal to it to heal our sickness or to solve our problems or to unleash our positive energies. Since humans are part of the Mind of God, they have divinity. Evil does not exist: it is mistaken for an error made by humans who do not understand that the material world is an illusion; and who do not realize that God's Mind is supreme and we are part of it, and that only good may come of it, in the long run, if we persevere. As one would expect, this is a very uplifting form of religion. It takes advantage of the medical fact that psychosomatic and even some physical illnesses may be cured if the patient has a strong faith in the cure, grounded in her faith in God. Unfortunately, there are many physical illnesses which cannot be cured by faith healing, leading to a host of tragic deaths, and to not a few legal challenges to the faith healing community.

Many Christian Scientists and New Thought religious followers would regard themselves as Christians, although their beliefs and religious practices do differ from those of mainstream Christianity. In particular they believe in Jesus as the first of the faith healers, and thus believe in all of Jesus's miracles. Their model for God is based on the New Testament God, but without the doctrine and dogma introduced by the Catholic Church from the 4th C. For example, sin does not exist in these new religions, and there is no sign of the angry God of retribution from the Old Testament.

According to Neusner, "*although God is commonly referred to in New Thought religion and sometimes personalized (as Father, Mother or Father-Mother), God is most fundamentally the Principle of Being – similar to Brahman in Hinduism. God is not a being himself, but rather the fundamental reality of the universe. God as Principle is at once the Law of creation, the Substance from which all things are made, and the Order that harmonizes the cosmos. Besides Mind, Law, Substance, and Order, numerous other synonyms for God express ideal and perfect states. Among those commonly used are Good, Truth, Love, Health, Life, Wisdom and Spirit. When it comes to matter (the material world) New Thought takes a less hostile stance than Christian Science. New Thought does recognize the material world, at least in its current state, as falling short of perfection. However, New Thought has traditionally believed that this material world can be uplifted, transformed and perfected.*"

If we rate Christian Science according to the six criteria of commonality among God models, we get the following. 1. There is only one reality, mind, the material world being an illusion; 2. There is one God who is mind, and humans are part of that mind; 3. Mind does not die when the body dies; 4. God is not a being, but the principle of being, at once the law of creation, the substance from which all things are made and the order which harmonizes the cosmos. He is love, good, truth, life, wisdom; 5. Humans follow the teachings of Jesus without the dogma and doctrine introduced by the Roman Catholic Church; 6. Humans appeal through their minds to the mind of God with which they are conjoined to heal sickness, and energize their lives.

So, when we say that God is mind, we need to be clear about what we mean by mind. One meaning is that mind and body are two separate entities, living in two different worlds, although connected. This is dualism, which is reflected in many traditional theistic beliefs. Another meaning is that only mind exists and that the physical world is an illusion, as believed by Hindus and Christian Scientists. Dualism was a concept formulated by philosopher Rene Descartes in the 17th C, and which still influences philosophy today. However, it has been largely discredited by advances in neuroscience which have clearly identified the role of the physical brain in providing the hardware for the mind, now seen as a software program (or more correctly, multiple programs) operating on the brain as platform (Jeeves). While we know *how* the brain computes (through neural circuits and synapses), and *why* (to produce behavior), we do not yet know about the step in between: *what* it computes (what neural codes and algorithms it uses) that leads to consciousness and cognition (see "The Future of the Brain" 2015, edited by Gary Marcus, paper by Matteo Carandini)). This computer analogy as a model for the mind raises an interesting question: has God found a way to get inside the brain to communicate with the mind? This idea will be developed in a later chapter and also in the concluding chapter. Bur first, we will look at the way in which God shares around his divinity in some religions.

Chapter 10

A God Who Shares Around His Divinity - Hinduism

M any religions have a God who shares around his divinity. Christianity has its Trinity of the three persons: the Father, the Son and the Holy Spirit within the one God. Then there are the angels, including the Angel Gabriel, and the apostles and the Pope and the saints, although it is the Roman Catholic Church, not God, who appoints the Pope and the saints. The ancient Jewish prophets also have a special place in the Christian world as God's messengers. In Islam, Muhammad enjoys a place second only to God as his last messenger or prophet. Abraham, Moses and Jesus also enjoy the position of God's messenger in Islam. Nonetheless, in these three religions God is undoubtedly supreme.

Hinduism, founded by Krishna 3,000 years ago in India, teaches of one ultimate reality, the God Brahman, who is manifest in many gods, some even playful. The God Krishna is the Creator, Vishnu the Preserver and Shiva the Completer, to name a few. Despite the multitude of gods, Hinduism is not strictly polytheistic. The Hindu believes that there are many pathways to the one God Brahman, and different individuals may take the pathway of the god suited to them. For example a philosopher type might envisage his God as an infinite being at the center of himself to be more meaningful. Another person, a religious type, may see God as a divine creator who watches over the world. Brahman can be seen in two ways, depending on whether the individual is philosophical or religious: as a transpersonal transcendent being or as a personal God.

According to Huston Smith, in his 1991 book entitled "The World's Religions", *"Hindus approach their God by suppressing the ego in order to open up to a wider world. This is not a matter of obliterating the ego, but rather it is about moving from the small limited self to the wider sphere of human existence and ultimately to God. It is an expansion of the self, and not a renunciation. The aim is to transcend the smallness of the finite self and to identify oneself with the transpersonal absolute; or shift to a personal God who is experienced as distinct from oneself."*

Hindus believe that the physical world is an illusion, and they seek ultimate reality or Brahman during their many lives. According to Smith, *"the word "Maya", describing the physical world, is translated in the West as "Illusion". However, this is not strictly accurate. It is more like a dream, which exists because we experience it, but it has no objective reality. The word in Hindi also has the sense of being tricky or magic."* Hindus believe in reincarnation and karma, that the sum of one's actions in this life and past lives affects one's fate in the next. One's early lives are lived as lower animals. With each successive death and reincarnation, provided the soul has done good things in its previous life, it has the opportunity of moving up the chain to higher animals, then into human form at the lowest caste level, and ultimately to the highest caste, called Brahmin, from which it is possible to reach ultimate reality or Brahman (or God, if you prefer that name). A Hindu thus needs to have the patience of a saint or the resignation of a Stoic to navigate this possibly never-ending cycle of life and death, before reaching Brahman. Although karma is deterministic, each soul has a choice in its life, i.e. it has free will; but its next life will be constrained or enhanced by that choice.

"Whereas Westerners accept experimentation or empiricism when it comes to the material world, they have difficulty applying the concept to the mind. Hindus have no such taboo. Through meditation involving the various schools of yoga they seek to suppress much of the actions of the body and the mind in order to move from the self to a transpersonal state" (Smith), which a Christian would call communing with God. By so suppressing the mind and body functions, this is to shut down much of the cerebral cortex where our thinking and intelligence resides, but also some of the parts of the brain associated with motor actions and the senses. This may allow signals to come through from more primitive parts of the brain, which we share with our animal cousins, which are normally swamped by the motor, sensory and conscious signals in the brain. These parts comprise the limbic system, which contains the hypothalamus, the hippocampus

and the amygdala, which is in contact with the pituitary gland and the hormonal system and the sympathetic and parasympathetic nervous systems, which affect the bodily emotions. The limbic system is also in contact with the pre-frontal lobe of the cortex, known to be active during religious experiences. It could be argued that this technique enables the subject to reach back to an earlier period of his life, or even his previous life, or his species, or the universe itself, with which his mind is interdependent and from which his body arose. This in order to find insights seated deep in his mind, possibly left there from earlier in human evolution. It is up to the reader to decide whether the alternate reality that Hindus experience during these trance-like meditations is real or only exists in the mind of the meditator. While there is much to learn by plumbing the depths of our uncorrupted minds and our primordial perspectives in order to find ultimate reality, this is not the direction that leads to the greatest achievements of humanity. These have occurred in music, art, mathematics, science and technology since the time when humans had acquired their full intelligence and culture through the higher order activity of the cerebral cortex in the brain. As pointed out for Buddhism, the trance-like state produced by yoga may be similar to those states arguably experienced by our distant ancestors, the hunter-gatherers, more than 50,000 years ago, through rhythmic dancing, chanting or singing to the beat of a drum.

If we rate Hinduism according to the criteria of commonality among God models we find the following. 1. There is only one reality, ultimate reality or Brahman (or God if you like), the material world being regarded as an illusion like in a dream; 2. There are many ways to Brahman, through many interventionist gods; 3. Hindus believe in reincarnation and karma, whereby the good done by a soul in one life determines the quality of the next; 4. Depending on the personality of the believer, God can be a transcendent being centered on the believer, or can be a personal God like the Christian God; 5. The law of karma ensures that Hindus lead a good life in this world; 6. Hindus seek to reach God through meditation and yoga, enabling them to reach deep into their minds to move from the small, limited self to the wider sphere of human existence and ultimately to God.

In the remainder of this chapter there follows a discussion of some of the newer religions, primarily those originating in America. Information for this discussion was sourced from Jacob Neusner's 2009 book entitled "World Religions in America". Readers are encouraged to consult this book for more details than can be included here.

There are religions in which God's reign in the heavens seems more diffuse. We have already met the God of Christian Science who is Mind, and who shares this Mind with humans. In the case of Theosophy, God is called the Solar Logos (that word again), and humans are each a divine spark and part of this God. Key components of this religion are the so-called Masters. The story goes that *"great religious leaders had been reincarnated numerous times before they reached their exalted status as prophets, saviors, visionaries, and saints. Over these lifetimes, the future Masters worked through the law of karma and pursued their spiritual evolution through occult studies until finally they became part of the divine hierarchy that rules and guides the evolution of the* earth" (Neusner). The reason for this diffuse divinity is that Theosophy is a syncretic religion. That is, it borrowed from earlier religions such as Hinduism and Buddhism. Hence its adherents' belief in reincarnation and karma. Although followers are not that close to Christianity they do believe that Jesus's rising from the dead validates their belief in reincarnation. *"Theosophy is classified as a metaphysical religion: its adherents believe in an alternative (spiritual) reality and spend their lives trying to unravel the mysteries of the universe and life and the origin of divinity; and to achieve their own spiritual evolution so that they may reunify with God"* Neusner). Theosophy does not have a lot of adherents today, but has given rise to hundreds of new religions.

The Baha'i faith, which originated in Iran, but is now worldwide, is another syncretic religion. *"Its adherents believe in one God, but that his revelations have been evolutionary and have encompassed all the religions of the world at different times and under different circumstances"* Neusner). The revelations at the time suited the particular social circumstances under which the receivers of these revelations were living. God's word has been revealed successively to Krishna, Confucius, Buddha, Moses, Zoroaster, Jesus, Muhammad and Baha'i's own prophet. The Baha'i strives for one world religion, world government and peace without racism. Since God has used so many prophets, championing so many different religions, then this is a model for God like no other. This religion is primarily about the real, physical world and the effect of God and his messengers upon it.

Scientology is a new and very successful American religion, which has attracted a lot of resistance from the religious establishments and the medical profession, the latter due to its opposition to psychiatry and psychology. It is a religion which holds that ultimate reality is composed of spirit rather than matter. In that sense it has borrowed from Hinduism. Its God is not like the Christian God, but rather is ultimate reality like the Hindu Brahman. According to Neusner, *"humans in their pure spiritual form are Godlike, and at the beginning of time, these spiritual humans, called "thetans", created the universe rather than did a supreme being such as a God. These thetans were reborn into the physical world with each generation of humans, and returned to the spirit world on the death of the human body which they inhabited. Thus, they have some similarity to the human soul of Christianity, except for the belief that the true nature of the human being is Godlike. The religious beliefs resemble those of Latter Day Saints' (Mormons') salvific belief in human progression towards a restored godlike status in the celestial worlds".* The repeated rebirth of thetans is similar to the reincarnation of Hinduism. *"Thetans are the individualized expressions of Theta, the cosmic source or life force."* In a sense, the Theta is like the Logos of the Stoics of the 3rd C BCE to the 1st CE, adopted by Philo into Judaism, and later by Christianity, which gave it a different meaning. The exact nature of God, or ultimate reality, is not defined by Scientology. Scientology is similar to Hinduism in recognizing a causal relationship between experiences of the present life and those of earlier incarnations. *"By a process of purification, adherents of Scientology may recapture their original thetan spiritual qualities, corrupted by the temptations and distractions of the physical world, and thus progress to become gods who live to infinity. The goal of salvation, infinite or immortal survival, can be achieved in this life by acquiring the knowledge and understanding of the basic operation of the universe. This requires intensive study, training and ritual practices in Scientology, not in science"* (Neusner). In this way the religion is similar to Asian religions that stress the development of highly disciplined practices, such as yoga and meditation, as a method for religious enlightenment. Once again, we see a resort to evoking the mysteries of the human mind. Apart from these practices, the moral code of Scientology is not unlike that of America generally, stressing liberty, equality and fraternity.

If we rate Scientology on the six criteria for commonality among models for God, we get the following. 1. Reality is composed of spirit rather than matter; 2. Scientologists believe in ultimate reality rather than a creator God, humans in their spiritual form being the creators of the universe; 3. Spiritual humans are reborn into the physical world with each generation, and return to the spiritual world on the death of the human body they inhabited; 4. There is a cosmic source or life force in place of a God, and humans are the individualized expression of this; 5. By a process of purification from the temptations of the material world, humans may eventually become gods and live to infinity; 6. Humans communicate with their spiritual selves through their minds by intense study and ritual, similar to meditation in eastern religions.

The Church of Latter Day Saints (the Mormons) is another American religion. It deals more with the physical world than the spiritual. *"Latter Day Saints believe in the Christian Trinity, but put their own spin on it. The biblical*

God is believed to have been a material being; and likewise Jesus Christ is envisioned as a corporeal person of flesh and bones; only the Holy Ghost is seen as a person of spirit. The Saints' God doctrine also includes a female deity: a Heavenly Mother. The Father God is the husband of this female deity, and she is the mother of all the pre-mortal spirits who become humanly embodied as earthly children. The Eternal Father God is supreme in ruling over a council of gods in the eternal world. The Christian Bible, especially the Old Testament, is the word of God. So too are the scriptures handed down by the founder of Latter Day Saints, Joseph Smith, in 1805, and the pronouncements of his successors as heads of the Church, down to the present day. Jesus Christ is to rule over the Kingdom of God on earth, at his second coming, for a thousand years before God's final judgement of humanity. This Kingdom will be physical and will be in the United States in Utah, which the Saints claim to be the promised land of the original Israelites. The Israelites are said to have migrated there before Christianity got underway in the Roman Empire, but were wiped out by ancestors of today's American Indians. Members of the Church may attain exalted Godlike status in the celestial (topmost) world by spiritual development through a knowledge of God, obeying his laws and participating in the prescribed rituals" (Neusner).

If we rate Mormonism according to the six criteria of commonality among models for God, we get the following. 1. For Mormons the material world is more important than the spiritual world; 2. There is one God who rules over a council of gods; 3. There is an afterlife in the future Kingdom of God, which will be on earth, in Utah; 4. God is a person, who once lived in material form; 5. God's laws are as laid down in the Bible and the writings of Joseph Smith and his successors; 6. Members of the church communicate with their God through their minds by intense study and rituals, as in eastern religions.

In this chapter we have looked at Hinduism, an ancient religion, and the newer religions of Christian Science, Theosophy, Baha'i, Scientology and the Church of Latter Day Saints, with respect to a God who shares around his divinity. The newer religions are all syncretic, in that they have borrowed from Judaism, Christianity, Hinduism and Buddhism, to come up with novel ideas for the divine, which have their own internal logic. Hinduism plays down the importance of the individual, while others give the human godlike status, provided he sticks to a strict regimen of study and/or meditation. God, for some of them, is personal; for others transpersonal. For some, he resides in the physical world; for others in the spirit world; and for the remainder, in both worlds. Some of the group try to orient themselves to science, or rather a pseudo-science. What they all have in common are rituals to call on the resources of the human mind in order to work through their faith. This may take the form of yoga, meditation, or intensive study. When we get to the concluding chapter, we will see how central is the human mind in any concept of a common thread underlying all religious experiences. But first we need to take a look at the religions which arose before Christ in a quarter of the world's population.

Chapter 11

China – Taoism and Confucianism

This survey of the models for God would not be complete without discussing the (historical) beliefs of one quarter of the world's population in China. This is a country which was largely isolated from the rest of the world for three millennia. In Christianity, Judaism and Islam, religion has provided, on the one hand, the moral and organizational basis for community cohesion and, on the other hand, the template for the religious experience. Whereas, in China these have been separate ever since the 6th C BCE. Confucianism has provided the moral basis of social cohesion and harmony and Taoism the template for religious or philosophical experience. Buddhism was a later non-indigenous entrant upon the scene from India in the 1st C CE. It has been discussed in a previous chapter.

Taoism

The model for God in Taoism shows remarkable similarities to Plato's transcendent God of the Forms, which provided the theoretical basis for the universe, and his immanent Demiurge which got things done in the real world. The transcendent sense of the Tao is: *"the ordering principle behind all life; the eternal law that structures the world; the ultimate reality (similar to the Hindu Brahman); the spirit of the universe"* (Smith). The immanent sense of the Tao is: *"the way of the universe; the driving power in all nature; vital energy".* There is a third sense of the Tao: it is *"the way of human life when it meshes with the Tao of the universe".* Note that Taoism, in its original form, does not have a personal God. Instead of the sense of a *transcendent God as* in Christianity, Taoism has the ultimate reality. Instead of the sense of the immanent God as in Christianity, Taoism has the *driving power in nature.* In fact, Taoism has a closer resemblance to Philo of Alexandria's Jewish concept of a *transcendent God* (to be discussed in a later chapter) who thought up the *Logos* that created the universe and through which all things were made. There is also a strong resemblance to a model for God which will be proposed in Chapter 15 and the appendix of this book. Taoism in practice also shows a strong resemblance to modern naturalism and environmentalism, in that man is expected to live in harmony with all creatures and the universe.

Taoism originated with a man named Lao Tzu, said to have been born in about 604 BCE, around the same time as Confucius (551 BCE). Taoism's bible is the *Tao Te Ching.* Taoism started out as a philosophy and a vitalizing program for the self. Influenced by Buddhism, a religious branch of Taoism developed around the time of Christ. It had churches and three divinities whom its adherents worshipped, one being the founder, Lao Tzu.

If we rate Taoism according to the six criteria of commonality among models for God we find the following. 1. Taoism deals with the material world. There is a transcendent sense of the Tao, the ordering principle behind all life, and an immanent sense, the driving power behind all nature; 2. There is no personal God in the original form of Taoism, rather there is ultimate reality; 3. There is no afterlife, only union with nature; 4. Taoism is a principle of being; 5. Taoism has a bible, the Tao Te Ching, which if followed will revitalize the self; 6. Taoists communicate with the Tao through their minds, suppressing the ego and approaching a state of peace into which the energy of the Tao can flow.

Taoism in practice resembles Hinduism and Buddhism, in suppressing the ego and thereby moving into an altered state of consciousness. This form of religious experience seems to enable the believer to reach back into the past of his life and even his species to find messages left there in earlier times, the vestiges of which have been preserved in his brain, and may emerge if they are not being swamped by conscious thinking and bodily functions.

Confucianism

Confucianism is the opposite of Taoism in that it steered man away from heaven and the cosmos and brought him down to earth, concentrating on achieving harmony among humankind. This was done through indoctrination of children from an early age with a moral code enshrined in Confucian proverbs, maxims and stories. The moral code originated with the family, and involved duty, honesty, modesty, respect, support and consideration. It was then extended to the community and to the whole of society. Confucius introduced this code during the warring states period in China in the 6th C BCE, when Chinese society was lawless and amoral. During the subsequent two millennia, Chinese civil servants were required to sit for examinations in Confucianism before being promoted to higher posts. Chinese society was a meritocracy during these times. We will not delve further into Confucianism here, as it does not provide a model for God; only a model for humanity. Those wishing for more information may consult Huston Smith's book "The World's Religions". The remarkable and enduring insight afforded by Confucianism is that you do not need God to achieve a moral order in society: Judaism, Christianity and Islam insist that you do!

As we have seen, in China, a moral code for the community developed separately to religion. This has tended to make each one pure in essence. The two have not been conflated, as in Islam in particular. This gives us an opportunity to study religious experiences in a form not biased by social pressures. In Taoism, we see emerge the same kind of religious experiences as in Hinduism and Buddhism, in that meditation and concentration enables the adherent to unshackle from the confines of the self and enter a wider world in which he can find peace. Once again the central role of the human mind in religious experiences is demonstrated. In the concluding chapter it will be shown how this gives a clue regarding a common thread underlying all religious experiences. But first, we need to discuss two opposing approaches to God, that of pessimism and optimism, and how pessimism plays out in two apocalyptic religions.

Chapter 12

A Pessimistic vs an Optimistic God

Considering that everyone lives on the same planet, it is remarkable how some religions, and their concept of humanity and the divine, are strongly pessimistic, while others are strongly optimistic. Into the former category we could place traditional Protestantism, especially Calvinism, Judaism and all the faiths which prophesy the end of the world in apocalypse, such as Seventh Day Adventists and Jehovah's Witnesses, to be discussed below. We could also include Buddhism and Stoicism, although the former does not have a God in its original form, and the latter was not really a religion. In the optimistic camp, we could include Taoists, Confucians, Hindus, Muslims, Roman Catholics, Transcendental Idealists, such as followers of Emerson, and the modern Christian faiths which downplay sin and concentrate on the spiritual and real-world growth of their flock. These include Unitarian, Evangelical, and Baha'i, Mormon, Scientology, Christian Science, New Thought and African American religions. Deism is realistic, rather than optimistic or pessimistic. We have described these various religions elsewhere, but for now will just illustrate their pessimistic or optimistic bent. Both optimistic and pessimistic religions share the belief that something is wrong and that it is necessary to appeal to a higher power to put it right. They just approach the matter with a different attitude. For a full discussion of the subject, readers are referred to William James's book "The Variety of Religious Experiences" (1902), and for apocalyptic faiths to "World Religions in America" by Jacob Neusner (2009).

A Pessimistic God

According to William James, the pessimistic point of view is that evil aspects of life are at its very essence, and that worldly meaning most comes home to us through maximizing the threat of evil instead of minimizing it. The problem with evil in Christian theology has stemmed from a monistic and pantheistic God who is All-in-All. This means evil is part of God. Yet, how can that be if he is all goodness? Better to have a pluralistic universe of which the devil is a part and can be expunged. There are some morbid-minded people for which evil is not a relation of the self to outside things, but is a vice inside the self, i.e. part of the person's nature which requires God's help to deal with it. This is the Germanic view as opposed to the Latin view of sin as just being part of a pluralistic world.

Those of the pessimistic persuasion believe that failure is the fate allotted. Pessimistic theologians hold failure to be essential and that only through the personal experience of humiliation which it engenders, can the deeper sense of life's significance be reached. Religious melancholy and conviction of sin played a large part in the history of Protestantism. It reflected the battle between the two kinds of self: carnal and spiritual.

The scientific belief in the eventual cold death of the universe (as implied by the second law of thermodynamics) demonstrates the ultimate futility of life in the physical world, according to the pessimistic point of view. Naturalism, Pantheism and Stoicism are obviously joyless because the world will end one day. Its followers know no joy in common with the followers of Hinduism, Islam and (optimistic) Christianity, who can point to a better life to come in the spirit world. The Stoic possesses a philosophy of despair; that nature's boons will yield to the ultimate fate, but one should be stoic in the meantime. This is a philosophy of resignation and fatalism.

Traditional Protestantism is the home of Bible-thumping preachers who promise hellfire and damnation to those in their congregations who do not mend their ways and follow the path of the Lord. Fear of eternal damnation is evoked. Humans are regarded as sinners at heart. *"Twice-born religions, requiring revival of the fallen sinner, tend to be pessimistic. Revivalist conversion always requires the subject first to be in great anguish. For the extremity of pessimism to be reached something more is required than observation of life and reflection on death. The individual must become in himself the prey of pathological melancholy"* (James). In this regard, traditional (protestant) Christianity is not as efficacious in curing sickness as it apparently was in Christ's time. This is because it tends to focus on the negatives such as guilt, sin and hell. Focusing on the negative is bad for the health.

Jews claim that their God originally chose them to shoulder the burden of living by his laws; and if they did so, he would look after them, his chosen people. The burden of the Jews has been a cross to bear indeed, from the exile in Babylon in the 6th C BCE, the conquest and subjugation of Israel by the Roman Empire in the 1st C BCE, the destruction of the Temple of Jerusalem in 70 CE, the later conquests by the Saracens, the Crusaders and the Ottoman Turks, the banishment from Spain in the middle ages, the pogroms in Russia in the 19th C, and worst of all the holocaust instigated by Nazi Germany during the Second World War. The God of the Jews would have to be classified as pessimistic, even though the Rabbis have been ingenious in finding meaning in God's punishments. Traditional Jews are ridden with guilt, and if there are catastrophes, they argue that God is punishing them for their sins against him. A typical comment from a Jew who has just experienced a misfortune is: "What have I done to deserve this?" Furthermore, many do not believe in an afterlife. Even more pessimistic are Seventh Day Adventists and Jehovah's Witnesses, who predict a coming apocalypse.

An Apocalyptic God

At least two American-made religions preach a coming apocalypse to coincide with Jesus' second coming and the Millennium (a thousand years of Jesus' rule). These are the Seventh Day Adventists and the Jehovah's Witnesses. The first calls itself Christian; the second does not. However both hold that the Bible is the word of God. The first has Jesus ruling from the spirit world; the second from earth.

The Seventh Day Adventists consider themselves to be Protestants and adopt most traditional Protestant beliefs about God and Jesus. They can be classified as evangelical conservatives. Generally their apocalyptic beliefs are derived from the New Testament, especially the Book of Revelation. "*According to this belief, when Jesus returns he will battle Satan and his followers, while Jesus' true believers, including the dead (who will have been resurrected), will ascend to meet him in the sky and then be lifted up to heaven. Unbelievers will be killed. Once in heaven, Jesus and his followers will reside there for the Millennium while the earth remains a lifeless wilderness. At the end of the thousand-year period, Jesus and his followers will return to earth, where there will be a final battle in which Satan is defeated. At this time the wicked will be resurrected to receive their final judgement, the earth will be cleansed by fire, annihilating evil forever, and then re-created by Jesus as an eternal paradise for his followers*" (Neusner). The second coming of Jesus is believed to be quite near.

On the other hand, Jehovah's Witnesses differ from Adventists and traditional Christians in their opposition to the Trinity and their conception of the nature and role of Jesus. Rather than the second person in the Trinity, "*Witness's believe that Jesus was the first of God's creations. He was not God, and on earth he was entirely human. God also created Satan who rebelled against him and became ruler of the world. This led to human sin, wickedness and death. To end Satan's reign, God sent Jesus, whose death was a sacrifice that allows eternal life for the steadfast in faith. Like Adventists, Witnesses believe in the judgement of the living and the dead at the time of Jesus' second coming. Those who have followed Jehovah (God) faithfully will be allowed to live, while those who have not will be annihilated in a great battle. Unlike the Adventist belief, those who have been accepted by Jesus will dwell on earth and restore it to the paradise it was prior to Satan's rule"* (Neusner). Witnesses are not shy about making predictions as to the date of the Second Advent. The first was 1914. When it did not occur, the date was revised to 1918, and then various other dates, the most recent being 1975.

Colorful though these stories and predictions may be, they are somewhat harsh on unbelievers, who will be killed in the apocalypse and ultimately be judged and sent to hell.

An Optimistic God

On the optimistic side, Taoists and Confucians both seek peace and harmony, which they believe can be attained. Hindus believe that the real world is an illusion, and seek ultimate reality or Brahman. They have many playful Gods as manifestations of Brahman and believe in reincarnation, which is cause for optimism if their karma is good, i.e. if they have led a kind life in prior incarnations. Roman Catholics celebrate life and God with festivals, rituals, sacraments, ceremonies, art, saints etc. The Roman Catholic practice of confession and absolution is a systematic method of keeping healthy-mindedness on top, and of starting again with a clean slate. Otherwise, focusing on remorse and guilt over sin will have negative mental effects. Sinners may have their sins forgiven by simply asking. There is more love and less fear of God in Catholicism. Evangelical Christians, who make up the bulk of American churchgoers, are optimistic and believe in salvation through Jesus's atonement for their sins. *"Martin Luther repudiated priestly absolution of sin as practiced in the Catholic Church. Yet, in the matter of repentance, he had some very healthy-minded ideas due to the largeness of his view of God. He held that sin may be inevitable. You should fight it, but not despair if it sometimes gets the better, because it is of the flesh; and God will forgive and focus on your good works. For Jesus died to atone for your sins"* (James).

The Baha'i religion is very optimistic. Its aim is world peace, the absence of racism and a common world religion encompassing all existing religions. Mormons have an optimistic view that humans are divine, and through devotion and study may reach their true potential. Christian Scientists and New Thought Religions believe that God is Mind (or Truth or Love or Peace) and we are part of that Mind and hence divine. We can appeal to that Mind to heal sickness or energize ourselves. Sin does not exist. It is only an aberration for those who do not realize that the physical world is an illusion and only Mind is real. *"These mind-cure religions give the convulsive self a rest, thus finding that a greater self is there. This involves relaxing and letting go. It is similar psychologically to the Lutheran justification by faith and the Wesleyan acceptance of free grace"* (James). Mind-cure religions are more successful than traditional Christianity in curing sickness because they focus on the positive: *God is with you, and you will get better.* These religions ignore the negatives such as hell and guilt. Even Catholicism, though largely optimistic, is too legalistic and moralistic to embrace the healthy-mindedness of the mind-cure religions.

Scientologists have a salvific belief in human progression towards a restored godlike status in the celestial worlds, and hence are optimistic. Like Hindus, they believe in reincarnation. African American religions arose from a belief that God would free them from bondage in this world or the next, thus identifying with the Israelites under the Roman yoke as described in the Bible. They sing God's praises accordingly. They started from a pessimistic appraisal of their then position, but looked forward to salvation with optimism.

The fact that optimistic and pessimistic religious experiences and models for God exist is a reflection of the dual nature of humanity. Some of us are born optimists and some born pessimists. Each will find the religion which best suits their own disposition. Optimism and pessimism in extreme form may become pathological, leading to mania and depression respectively. These conditions are sometimes caused by imbalances of dopamine and serotonin in the bloodstream, which can have an effect on the brain. Once again, we see the human brain, and hence mind, being central to religious experiences. This connection will become clearer in following chapters. The next chapter examines the possibility of the mind of humanity forming a union with God.

Chapter 13

Humans Evolving Towards a Union with God

There is a school of thought that the ultimate endpoint of human evolution is to achieve a level of excellence sufficient to form a union with God. Whether a flawed humanity will ever reach such a state of grace is a debatable point. If it did then this would only be through the triumph of good over evil, of love over hatred and of intelligence over ignorance. Such a model was proposed by Jesuit priest and paleontologist Teilhard de Chardin, who believed in evolution, with the result that his books were banned by the Catholic Church. If humanity could form a union with God in the future it tells us something about the kind of God that might be

To be clear, de Chardin was not proposing the evolution of a new species to displace man. Rather he postulated that the human body and brain had evolved as far as they could go, but the human mind was capable of further evolution through networking of all the minds on the planet. He proposed this in 1951, before the advent of personal computers and the internet. At that time, he did not attract a large number of followers, but today it is easier to imagine such a network, so his ideas are worth revisiting. He was not proposing that the individual human mind would evolve further. Rather, he was talking about the networked mind of humanity. Humans would still retain their individual minds and identities but there would be a super mind on a higher level to which they would all contribute, each according to their ability. A holistic mind could thus emerge from everyone being connected to the network through their personal computers, for example. The cross-linking that this would provide would be analogous to the 2000 cross-links between every one of the 100 billion neurons, or electrical pathways, in our brains, which is said to be responsible for our consciousness and our ability to outthink a computer where lateral thinking and insight are required. Could this lead to the evolution of some kind of higher level consciousness of humanity, or a super mind, on the planet, which in some respects would be analogous to a god? As such, it may be able to form a union with the real God. De Chardin argues that for this networked mind of humanity to approach a union with God, then God must already exist (and must be compatible with this network of human minds). Of course, we are a long way from this point. Up to now digital networking has been used largely for trivial pursuits, averaging down intelligence rather than boosting it.

Physicist Frank Tipler makes a case for the evolution of intelligence in the universe to approach an Omega point, at which time it would become a kind of god. In this he is in line with other physicists, who argue that a super intelligent God does not yet exist, and the only prospect for one is for intelligence to continue to evolve on earth and thence into the universe. In my book "God in The Time of The Internet", I explore this long shot on the basis of de Chardin's network of human minds, achieved through the internet and complemented by, but not replaced by, super computers. This is all science fiction at the present time, but science fiction sometimes has a habit of coming true, given enough time and sufficient new knowledge and technology.

One shortcoming of such a super intelligence is that it may lack any emotional or moral qualities, and thus would fall short of what is required in a God. What's more, the odds are against it ever coming to fruition without love and morality. In a world full of weapons of mass destruction and with the penchant for violence in disaffected groups, no doubt inherited from survival of the fittest during evolution, we may not last even one hundred years, let alone long enough for a super mind to exist. On the bright side, it may be possible for positive emotions and morality to be taken up by a super mind, through programming these characteristics into the devices and computers which act as gateways into the network. Hackers would need to turn their considerable talents to this instead of to making mischief.

As far-fetched as such ideas may be, forming a union with God is a feature of Mormonism and Christian Science.

In the former, this may occur across the boundary between the physical and spiritual worlds; in the latter in the world of mind, as Christian Scientists regard the physical world as an illusion. The union described by de Chardin takes place between a network of human minds, based on a platform of interconnected physical human brains, and a God in the spiritual world. In this, and in Mormonism, we see a suggestion of God or the Holy Spirit reaching from the spiritual world into the physical world to communicate with humans through their brains, and hence their minds. This is a further pointer to the importance of the human mind in religious experiences. In Chapter 17, we will ask the question that previous chapters have been leading up to. Is God within the human mind? But first we must take a look at the formal theology of Christianity.

Chapter 14

Formal Theology of Christianity

1. The Christian Trinity

The Christian doctrine of the Trinity maintains that there is one, and only one, God who exists in three distinct persons: God the Father; God the Son; and God the Holy Spirit. The Trinity was formally stated in the Nicene Creed of CE 325, and entrenched at the Council of Chalcedon in 451, with the purpose of enjoining all the divine beings mentioned in the Bible as the one God. The Trinity has caused much discussion, argument and schism over the centuries within the monotheistic world. Muslims do not accept it, and do not accept Jesus as being God, or for that matter the son of God. They regard Jesus as a prophet, like Muhammad, but Muhammad to be the last, and most relevant, prophet. The Jews likewise do not accept the divinity of Jesus, but regard him as yet another prophet. Even within the Christian Church, there is a difference in emphasis with respect to the Trinity from the Western (later Roman) Church and the Eastern (later Orthodox) Church. The former holds that the Holy Spirit, in proceeding both from the Father and the Son, unites them in a single Godhead. Whereas the latter maintains that both the Son of God and the Holy Spirit proceed from the Father, who is thus the single source of both. This is seen by the Churches as a non-trivial difference, and is symptomatic of how the mystery of the Trinity has caused so much confusion among Christians.

One theory about the motivation behind the formulation of the Trinity is that it would capture the love that the three persons in God felt for each other, Christianity being based on love; which could then be extended to humans. However, it is more likely that the motivation was to bestow divinity on Jesus. This was important to the Christian religion, it being based in large part on his teachings and life. However, it opened up a number of logical flaws. For example, how can God be both himself and his son? Is it not a contradiction in terms for a god to take mortal form? Shouldn't he only exist in the spirit world? To put a modern genetic spin on it, if God impregnated Jesus's mother Mary, then Jesus would derive half his chromosomes from God and half from Mary. If so, then he cannot be identical with God, his father. Half of him has mortal origins from his mother. Of course, if God had planted an embryo into Mary's uterus, which was a clone of himself, then it would have been possible for Jesus to have used Mary as a surrogate mother, and not have any of her chromosomes. However, the state of medical science was not sufficiently advanced for early Christians to have thought of this explanation.

The Holy Spirit (or Holy Ghost in some texts) seems redundant. If God resides in the spirit world, then why does he need another person in that world just to impregnate Mary and to do all those other things the Holy Spirit was supposed to have done? Why could God not have done them himself?

There is a logical alternative to the usual interpretation of the Trinity, which however was not contemplated by the Church. God the Father could be the transcendent God who created the universe and all its laws; God the Holy Spirit could be the immanent God who makes things happen within the real world, like impregnating Mary. Jesus could have been a prophet sent by God and the Holy Spirit to earth with special powers, but in human form, to let us know what God expects of us in terms of behavior, to keep us on the right path. Otherwise we would continue to go the way we had evolved to be, through survival of the fittest, with its associated violence and acquisitiveness; which though necessary for us to have arrived in this world, had left us with a morality contrary to God's law and not in the best interests of our continued survival as a species in a world of massed armies.

The ancient Greek philosopher, Plato, who lived in the period covered by the Old Testament, proposed two Gods: the (transcendent) God of the Forms, who provided the laws of nature and the commensurate potentialities for the universe; and the Demiurge, the immanent God who made things happen in the real world, consistent with the Forms. God the Father could be equated to Plato's God of the Forms; and the Holy Spirit to Plato's Demiurge; and Jesus to Plato's philosopher-king.

2. A Transcendent vs an Immanent God

Does God transcend time, or act within time? For indeed, if time commenced with the Big Bang, then nothing could have preceded it, presumably not even God. So if God is put forward as the first cause who created the universe through the Big Bang, then such a God must have been timeless, that is existing outside time. In other words, he created the universe *with* time rather than *in* time. Then we are left with the riddle of how a timeless God can drive events in the real world which exists in time? A related question is whether God is transcendent, that is existing above, other than and distinct from the universe; or is he immanent, and thus always and only present within the universe? Or is he both? For to affirm God's transcendence and to deny his immanence is to arrive at deism. To deny his transcendence and affirm his immanence is to arrive at pantheism.

The question we must address is whether it is possible for God to both create the universe and be part of his creation. The easy answer is that he is God, so he can do anything he wants. However, if we wish to base our belief on some sort of logic, this simply will not do. Sure, it is possible for a king to create a city outside his domain, and then to rule over it. However, this king is acting within the one world and within time. A transcendent God would be doing neither. As we have just discussed, Christianity puts forward a framework in the Trinity, which goes some way towards solving this riddle, although this was never the intention. God the Father could be the transcendent God who created the universe, and God the Holy Spirit could be the immanent God who acts within the universe in time. In the Bible, the two are used interchangeably, but in terms of the big issues, God the Father is the creator and the Holy Spirit is the one who impregnated Mary, who gave birth to Jesus.

What does it mean to be transcendent and timeless? The Oxford dictionary defines transcendent, in the sense of Kantian philosophy, as meaning: *not realizable in experience; existing apart from, not subject to limitations of the material universe.* Whereas the word transcendental, is defined as: *a priori character presupposed in and necessary to experience.* A transcendent God is meant to possess both these qualities. What are some mundane examples which may be considered to be transcendent? Laws in pure mathematics are truths which would exist even without a material world. They may not have much application in a non-material world, but they could still exist. Thus they are transcendent.

For God to be immanent, he must exist within his creation, to be nearby to us all, and to use his powers to shape the world. In other words, he must be able to act within time. Thus we have a paradox of God being both in space and time and outside space and time. The Bible ignores this paradox and unashamedly declares that God is both immanent and transcendent. He is both *"nearby"* and *"far away"*, according to Jeremiah 23:23. God's immanence is referred to in Colossians 1:17. *"In him all things hold together"*. God's transcendence is referred to in Isiah 55:9. *"As the heavens are higher than the earth, so are my ways higher than your ways and my thoughts than your thoughts"*.

Thus, to believe in the traditional Judeo-Christian God, one must accept that he is both transcendent and immanent.

Christianity does show a way out of this paradox, with the birth of Jesus, as the son of God. As Jesus took mortal form, he was clearly immanent in the world. So was the Holy Spirit who impregnated Mary. This would leave the Father to be transcendent. It seems that whatever the nature of one's belief in a single God, this God must possess both transcendent and immanent characteristics. Otherwise, he is not really a God. In the case of a Deist, he believes in a transcendent God who created the universe and the laws of physics, and then let them go to it, independently of him. Surely for the Deist this would mean that an immanent God takes the form of the laws of physics and whatever other natural forces are required to move things along? On the other hand, the Pantheist believes in nature as being the immanent God who emerged at the Big bang and caused everything thereafter; the Pantheist is silent on what caused the Big Bang, or just assumes it was spontaneous, coming out of nothing.

3. God as First Cause

If God is the First Cause of the universe, as stated by the great theologian Cardinal Newman, then his attributes can be derived from formal theology. I paraphrase Newman's words below, as quoted in William James' book on p 479. If you get lost in the metaphysical logic, you won't be the first, nor the last. So, first a word of introduction. Religion, like philosophy, must answer questions that society does not frame; but unlike philosophy it must infuse all of life with motive. Religious intention looks to the future. It is important for faith. The Scholastics wrote: "It is more important to love God than to know him". They meant that the intention itself, rather than the clarity of the object, distinguishes the religious sentiment. On the other hand, Newman wrote:

> God differs from all his creatures in possessing existence in and of itself. From this, theology deduces by mere logic most of his other perfections. For instance he must be both necessary and absolute, cannot not be and cannot in any way be determined by anything else. This makes him absolutely unlimited from without and unlimited also from within; for limitation is non-being and God is being itself. This being unlimited makes God infinitely perfect. Moreover, God is one and only, for the infinitely perfect can admit no peer. He is spiritual, for were he composed of physical parts, some other power would have to combine them into the total, and his existence in and of itself would thus be contradicted. He is therefore both simple and non-physical in nature. He is simple metaphysically also, that is to say his nature and his existence cannot be distinct, as they are in finite substances which share their formal natures with one another, and are individual only in their material aspect. Since God is one and only this excludes from his being all those distinctions, so familiar in the world of finite things, between potentiality and actuality, substance and accidents, being and activity, existence and attributes. We can talk, it is true, of God's powers, acts and attributes, but these discriminations are only virtual, and made from the human point of view. In God all these points of view fall into an absolute identity of being.
>
> This absence of all potentiality in God obliges him to be immutable. He is actuality through and through. Were there anything potential about him, he would lose

or gain in its actualization, and either loss or gain would contradict his perfection. He cannot, therefore, change. Furthermore, he is immense, boundless, for could he be outlined in space, he would be composite, and this would contradict his indivisibility. He is therefore omnipresent, indivisibly there at every point of space. He is similarly wholly present at every point in time – in other words eternal. For, if he began in time, he would need a prior cause, and that would contradict his existence as being in and of itself. If he ended, it would contradict his necessity. If he went through any succession, it would contradict his immutability.

He has intelligence and will and every other creature perfection, for we have them, and he must be greater than us. In him however, they are absolutely and eternally in act, and their object, since God can be bounded by naught which is external, can primarily be nothing else but God himself. He cannot be called "free" internally within himself, with the freedom of contrariness that characterizes finite creatures. Externally, however, or with respect to his creation, God is free. He cannot need to create, being in happiness already. He wills to create then by an absolute freedom.

Being thus a substance endowed with intellect and will and freedom, God is a person; and a living person also, for he is both object and subject of his own activity, and to be this distinguishes the living from the lifeless. He is thus absolutely self-sufficient: his self-knowledge and self-love are both of them infinite and adequate and need no extraneous conditions to perfect them.

He is omniscient, for in knowing himself as First Cause he knows all creature things and events by implication. His knowledge is with foresight, for he is present to all time. Even our free acts are known beforehand to him, for otherwise his wisdom would admit of successive moments of enrichment, and this would contradict his immutability. He is omnipotent for everything that does not involve logical contradiction. He can make being – in other words his power includes creation. If what he creates were made of his own substance it would have to be infinite in essence as that substance is; but it is finite; so it must be non-divine in substance. If it were made of a substance, an eternally existing matter, for example, which God found there to his hand, and to which he simply gave its form, that would contradict God's definition of First Cause, and make him a mere mover of something caused already. The things he creates then, he creates out of nothing, and gives them absolute being as so many finite substances in addition to himself. The forms he imprints upon them have their prototypes in his ideas. But as in God there is no such thing as multiplicity, and as these ideas for us are manifold, we must distinguish the ideas as they are in God and the way in which our minds externally imitate them. We must attribute them to him only in a terminative sense, as differing aspects, from the finite point of view, of his unique essence.

God of course is holy, good and just. He can do no evil, for he is positive being's fullness, and evil is negation. It is true that he has created physical evil in places, but only as a means of wider good. Moral evil he cannot will, either as end or means, for that would contradict his holiness. By creating free beings he permits it only, neither his justice nor his goodness obliging him to prevent the recipients of freedom from misusing his gift.

As regards God's purpose in creating, primarily it can only have been to exercise his absolute freedom by the manifestation to others of his glory. From this it follows that the others must be capable in the first place of knowledge, love, and honor, and in the second place of happiness, for the knowledge and love of God is the mainspring of happiness. In so far forth one may say that God's secondary purpose in creating is love.

Three comments can be made about the above paragraphs. First, while these metaphysical aspects of God's nature may be of great interest to theologians, according to James and Allport, the average Christian in prayer would not delve so deeply into the matter. It is sufficient that he respects his God and can communicate with him and receive comfort and solace and encouragement from him. Secondly, since God is unlimited in every dimension and mode he is basically indefinable. For how can we define anything which has no limits, since we are only observing part of it? This concept of an indefinable God is also found in formal Islam and in the Hindu concept of Brahman or ultimate reality. Thirdly, this theological model for God may be a house of cards built on unstable ground, for the assumption in all of it is that God is First Cause. But what if he is not? What if the Big Bang is First Cause, and it arose spontaneously out of nothing, in a quantum fluctuation, as some leading physicists contend (Hawking)? In the next chapter we will examine this idea and its implications for a model of God based on a non-thinking, non-personal First Cause.

Before that, let us recap what has gone before. It is important for those Christians seeking meaning and logic to support their faith, to have an understanding of the Trinity, of God's transcendence and immanence, and of his attributes which follow from his proposed role as First Cause. In this chapter we have looked at these from both an unconventional and a conventional theological perspective. These perspectives will be utilized in the concluding chapter which attempts to find a common thread underlying all models for God.

Chapter 15

God as a Non-thinking First Cause or Teleology

There is a tendency among modern Christians to envisage God in some non-human form, rather than the anthropomorphic God of the Catholic Church, which pictures him as an old man seated in the clouds. There was a very early attempt by a Jewish theologian to break away from this anthropomorphic model for God. It arose out of the drive to reconcile the Hebrew Torah (which subsequently became the Biblical Old Testament) and Greek philosophy in the 1st C CE. This took place in Alexandria at the time of the Roman Empire, but a time when Greek learning dominated intellectual life. Philo was a Jewish theologian familiar with both the Torah and Greek philosophy. He adapted to Jewish theology a concept called the "Logos", which originated with Plato, 4 centuries earlier, and had been adopted by the Greek Stoics, among whose followers were several Roman Emperors. Logos is Greek for "word", but philosophers loaded it with the meaning of "reason" or "wisdom". The Stoics believed it was the divine animating principle pervading the universe, from which all things were made. *"Philo held that the Logos originated from an indefinable transcendent God, who thought up the idea of the Logos and then implemented it to create and sustain the universe"* (Wright). This was seen as a way to solve the paradox of God being above and separate from the world (transcendent) but at the same time active within the world (immanent). Thus God the transcendent came up with the Logos, which was then set to work on the universe. Since the Logos was an invention, and therefore an extension, of God, then there was a continuity between the two. The logos was directional, and had a purpose: to create the universe and man, but it was not anthropomorphic. Rather it was a kind of algorithm or rather a series of algorithms, like a computer program. Philosopher Robert Wright, in his 2009 book, called it the Divine Algorithm. Making use of the laws of science the Logos created and sustained the universe in a way which led to the evolution of man, and then imbued man with morality and reciprocal altruism (according to Wright) to ensure his continued existence. *"Thus a cosmic wisdom became seamless with a human wisdom (which in Philo's world, emanated from the words of the Torah, especially Proverbs)"*. In this way, the Logos, an invention and extension of God, created man, and in so doing had ensured that channels of communication remained open back to God. Just how this could have been done will be discussed in the concluding chapter.

As a postscript, the author of the Gospel of John, written within the next 50 years after Philo, adapted the Logos to Christianity, but it was translated from the Greek as "word", not "reason" or "wisdom": "*In the beginning was the word, and the word was with God, and the word was God*" (John 1:1). In John, Jesus was cast as the incarnate Logos, from which all things were made.

Let us try to construct such a model of an indefinable transcendent God and his Logos as Philo did, but with the benefit of modern science, unknown in Philo's time. Let us first substitute a non-thinking transcendent God for Philo's God. Then let us define the transcendent God as: *one, but for which nothing could be or be conceived to be* – one who harbors the Transcendental Truth about the potentialities of the universe. The definition of *Transcendental* in the Oxford dictionary, in the Kantian philosophical sense, is: *a priori character, presupposed in and necessary to experience.* In looking at our model for the Logos, next we must distinguish between a scheme in which the universe is moved along according to some prior cause or design, and one in which it finds its own way forward based on some sort of selection of the best of available options. In the former, the outcome is pre-determined, and this concept resembles Deism with a non-thinking God. In the case of the latter, the outcome is not pre-determined by some prior design or cause, but occurs through some sort of creative, but self-driving process, the end result of which is greater complexity, ultimately leading to the evolution of the human being. These two cases are not atheism because they require something more than just the laws of physics and chance. They need an overriding Transcendental Truth and are directional.

The first scheme implies a deterministic world in which every event and every outcome is already fixed from the first cause or prior design. Astrology, which links the events during our lives to the positions of the stars at our birth, fits into this scheme. So does the Newtonian model in physics that everything must have a cause. Since all the causes of the present are in the past and all the causes of the future are in the present, there is nothing that can be done to alter the future. Likewise, the design or purpose of the universe would already be fixed. If we were to know everything about the present, according to this model, then we would know everything about the future. The only reason we are surprised by unexpected events is that there is some hidden cause we were not aware of.

As an aside, if this model applies to the universe, does it also apply to our lives? The strict behaviorists would say that it does. According to them our behavior in a particular situation is pre-determined by our genetic make-up, our prior training and the events around us, especially human events. Since these are either fixed or beyond our control, we can do nothing about them. What we regard as free will is not free will at all. We might think we have free will, but really we have been programmed to behave in a certain way in a given situation. The reader may not accept this model, but this is what determinism means. We will shortly look at a non-deterministic world, when we discuss that model for God. But first let us pursue determinism further.

There are two sub-types of determinism: causative and teleological. Causative means that there is a first cause, and then everything after that follows inevitably in a causal chain, consistent with the laws of physics. This is self-explanatory.

The Greek philosopher Aristotle taught teleology. This is different to causation. Teleology is the view that developments are due to the purpose or design that is served by them. This is the doctrine of final causes. Aristotle would have argued that humans were meant to appear on the planet, and that all developments in the universe up to now were leading up to this outcome. He believed everything and everyone had a purpose, according to some pre-existing design. One could call this design "God" or "nature". It does not originate from a designer: it just exists as a brute fact. If we say there was a designer, then we would stray into Deism.

Let us consider what the causative and teleological models for God or the Logos mean. They imply that once the Big Bang occurred, the birth of the galaxies and stars and planets were all a foregone conclusion. So too were the development of a life-sustaining environment on planet earth, the occurrence of first life, the evolution of life from single-cell creatures to human beings, the evolution of the human brain, and the appearance of you and me on this planet.

What is it that could bring about this deterministic outcome in the causative, as opposed to the teleological, model? For one, the initial conditions at the Big Bang, which set up an expanding universe. Then we have the laws of physics, which determine what will happen thereafter within this expanding universe. All the matter and energy in the universe is bound to behave according to these laws. Once the Big bang occurred, the causal chain was set in motion. It was then inevitable, according to this deterministic model, that the earth would form and life would evolve and you and I would be born.

We come at the end of a very long causal chain stretching in time over the 14 billion years since the Big Bang. Some of these events had a low probability of coming about, but given enough time, they may have been bound to occur somewhere in the universe. What then are the main components of this causal chain? First was the formation and expansion of hydrogen and helium after the Big Bang, then their coalescence into galaxies. Out of these galaxies, stars were born. In the center of giant stars, the life-giving element carbon was created by nuclear fusion. These giant stars became unstable and exploded in supernovae, spreading carbon and the heavy elements to the far corners of the universe, where some of them were drawn into the orbit of our sun, and aggregated to form planets. One planet developed a life-sustaining environment with carbon, water, an oxygen atmosphere and some essential heavy elements. Amino acids, the building blocks of proteins, were synthesized from these ingredients. Life began in this primeval soup. Single-cell creatures evolved into complex life forms, at the apex of which was the human being with his advanced brain. The great mystery is: how ever could this little island of complexity develop out of an immense and chaotic universe which, according to the second law of thermodynamics, is slowing down, using up its energy and becoming less ordered? Paradoxically, the second law would not be violated by a local increase in complexity so long as the universe on the whole, in aggregate, was still becoming less ordered. So, was it inevitable, by the laws of probability, that, given enough time, at least one island of complexity would develop in the universe? Having powers of observation and intelligence, we are aware that this has happened at least once, as we are here to tell the tale.

For this to happen, there must have been a potentiality for it all along, given the initial conditions at the Big Bang and the laws of physics. But what drew our part of the universe into this outcome? Was it just something which was bound to happen somewhere in the universe, by the laws of probability, given enough time? Or was there some quality, principle, force or algorithm – some teleology - working behind the scenes, increasing the probability enormously for such an unlikely chain of events? For example, in a different model than presented here, physicist Paul Davis has suggested that God is a personification of some mythical quality with a transcendent reality, such as economy, symmetry or harmony, which sets the direction for the universe and steers at least part of it towards greater complexity. In my book "God in The Time of The Internet" I proposed a universal algorithm, or rather a series of such algorithms, which exist and which can steer complex outcomes within the universe, such as the evolution of life by natural selection. This would be a natural algorithm. However, we are more familiar with manmade algorithms such as those that drive the software in a computer or those procedures which carry out long division. Any repetitive procedure which leads to a solution is called an algorithm. So, in summary, the deterministic models deem that at the time of the Big Bang, the probability of humans ultimately arriving was 1. That is: it was a certainty.

On the contrary, if our arrival on this planet depended only on the probability of a chain of unlikely events, then the case can be made that there was no certainty that it would turn out the way it did. It may never have reached completion or it might have gone another way. In such a model, at the time of the Big Bang, the probability of our arriving would have been less than 1. This is the non-deterministic model for the Logos.

To understand this concept, let us do a little thought experiment. Imagine, that at the time of the Big Bang, the coming evolution of the universe and life could not have been foreseen. That is to say, at that time, the chain of events that would have led ultimately to the appearance of humans somewhere in the universe in the 14 billion years after the Big Bang, had a combined probability, based on the laws of physics, of less than 1. Let's say much less than 1, say 0.001. Yet we did arrive on earth! So, how can this be reconciled without invoking a theistic thinking God? The only conclusion is that, in a non-deterministic world, we arrived here through a series of lucky chances. Sure, some kind of underlying quality, principle, force or algorithm might have helped things along, over and above the laws of physics, but the probability at the outset would have been less than 1. So, this (non-deterministic) model for a non-thinking god falls short of what we would expect a god (or a logos) to be. If it were a god, our eventual arrival on the planet would have been a certainty from the beginning, not some long shot chance. As Albert Einstein once famously said: "God does not play dice with the universe". However, just because this model does not shape up as a god, does not mean it is wrong. Perhaps this is the true state of affairs. To compensate for not having a god, humans would have gotten free will, which is only possible in a non-deterministic world.

The big difference between the deterministic and non-deterministic models for the Logos becomes apparent when we consider the future. The deterministic model has no room for human free will. However the non-deterministic model allows humans to intervene in their own future, in ways not embedded already in the causal chain or teleological endpoint. We can shape the future through using our intelligence, and explore the best way forward. The future is not a foregone conclusion, but depends on the free choices we make. These can involve moral and ethical considerations rather than resorting to survival of the fittest which has driven evolution up to now. By using our intelligence we may be able to avoid self-destruction and extinction, if that is the way things are otherwise headed.

The atheistic model for the universe differs from the above two types of model for the Logos in that the probability of the Big Bang leading to the eventual arrival of humans after 14 billion years is based solely on the laws of physics. This model does not need to invoke any non-thinking God - any Transcendental Truth - setting the scene; nor any Logos based on an underlying quality, principle, force or algorithm driving things along, let alone a thinking God. However, without their help, life may have had little chance of coming to be. So, our arrival on earth, according to this atheistic model, was a very, very lucky chance. We made it, but we may well not have.

As an aside, in recent times in America, there have emerged certain nature religions such as Neopaganism, which have no sentient God in the traditional sense. These celebrate the oneness of humanity with all of nature. This is a form of Pantheism – a belief that nature, the universe, life and humanity are all God. This is not the same as a non-thinking first cause and teleology described above, which set the course and *steer* nature rather than *are* nature. Nature religions hark back to the animism of primitive times in which humans worshipped certain natural entities such as the sun and the moon, mother earth, and the female goddess of fertility, imbuing them with spiritual properties (in the absence of knowledge about their natural causes). Yet, with the benefit of hindsight, to worship such things seems a contradiction in terms. If events occur by natural causes then they are not spiritual but are of the real, material world. So, why worship them? This incorrect labelling has occurred because the believers in Neopaganism and Pantheism wanted to turn them into religions; but inconveniently, by definition, religion must deal largely or exclusively with the spirit world.

The purpose of this chapter has been to explore models for the universe which do not require a thinking God as creator and driver, but rather a non-thinking Transcendental Truth, a stand-alone First Cause (the Big Bang) and a driving Teleology consisting of a series of natural algorithms. These models imply that the universe and life were not planned or designed, but rather were merely *meant to be*. The models will become important in the Appendix, where an attempt will be made to find the underlying common thread beneath all religious experiences, using a teleological model as creator of the universe. But first let us look at the Atheist's alternative to God.

Chapter 16

The Atheist's Alternative to God

A theists do not believe in the existence of a supernatural world, let alone an interventionist God who watches over us and listens to our prayers. They can be found among the approximately 25% of the population who have never had a religious experience of the type described in Chapter 2. As such, they are likely to be "left-brain" people who are conceptually orientated, as opposed to "right-brain" people who are more into art and human relationships. About 1% of citizens from the United States report that they are Atheists. However, the number is likely to be higher due to reluctance to be labelled as an Atheist in a predominantly religious country.

Some of the most intelligent individuals who have ever lived are or were Atheists. These include cosmologist Stephen Hawking, philosopher Bertrand Russell, mathematician Alan Turing and psychologist Sigmund Freud, along with many Nobel Prize Laureates. As such, we cannot ignore them. They may be right! Albert Einstein was a Pantheist rather than an Atheist, but he did not believe in a sentient God. Many Atheists believe that the bad side of religion outweighs the good side, especially when religion is combined with ignorance, bigotry, small-mindedness, extremism and vilification. Many psychological problems have been attributed to guilt generated by religion. Be that as it may, Atheists have to contend with the fact that in the United States, 90% of the population say that they believe in God, and of those, 75% have religious experiences which they attribute to the presence of God, although these numbers are coming down in Northern Europe. Given that an Atheist does not believe in the existence of God, what is he or she to make of the religious experiences of believers described in this book? Believers certainly accept these experiences as real. Furthermore, as described in Chapter 2 and the concluding chapter of this book, there is scientific evidence that these religious experiences, whether they indicate the presence of God or not, have a biological as well as a cultural basis.

Since the beliefs of Atheists and Theists are irreconcilable, this book will take a dual approach and present its conclusions to religious people within their frame of reference and to Atheists, within theirs. In the next two chapters, where the expression "God in the mind" or "a faculty in the mind to access what is believed to be a God" is used it refers to what believers accept as real as an article of faith. An Atheist might see this as a psychological phenomenon conditioned by religious indoctrination and based on some innate predilection to believe in the supernatural, wired into our brains, which was adaptive during evolution. Alternatively, he may see it as a meme originating in our distant past and passed on culturally from one generation to the next due to the survivability benefits it bestowed; although the evidence in this book suggests religiosity is at least partly genetically determined. The Appendix attempts to mount a case in terms acceptable to an Atheist or a person who does not believe in a sentient God.

What a religious person would regard as real, an Atheist would consider as coming from the imagination. This is the very imagination which enabled us to evolve into what we are today. It gave us a tremendous survivability advantage as it enabled humans to envisage scenarios; to be able to anticipate where a predator may be lurking or an enemy may be waiting in ambush. This imagination has been essential for innovation of all kinds, including technological and scientific invention. Why should it not be used to envisage the supernatural, if that is what is desired by the individual?

In the remainder of this chapter, the Atheist case will be put as best as possible, and guidance given as to what an Atheist is to make of the evidence in this book that religious experiences in some people may have a biological basis.

Evolutionary biologist Richard Dawkins, in his book "The God Delusion" states that the scriptures are *as likely to be true as stories about fairies living at the bottom of the garden*. Many other Atheists share this view, given scientific and historical errors in the Bible. They do not believe in the story of Genesis, as it is invalidated by geological and fossil evidence and radioactive dating, which confirm the age of the earth to be in the billions of years, not 6,000 years as claimed in the Bible. Unlike Deists, traditional Christians and Muslims, Atheists do not believe that some invisible God designed and created the universe. The Big Bang and the laws of science are all that is required to explain the evolution of the universe and the coming of life, humans and intelligence to our planet. God was not the First Cause; rather it was the Big Bang. And what caused the Big Bang? It happened spontaneously. It had no cause. It was the First Cause. It could have arisen out of nothing through a quantum fluctuation, with the positive matter and energy created being offset by the negative energy of gravity as the universe expanded (Hawking). Alternatively, some scientists say that the Big bang might have arisen out of a black hole in another universe, or as the result of a former universe collapsing in on itself under the force of gravity into a Big Crunch (Davies). No one knows how it occurred. That is still scientific speculation. However there is strong evidence that it did occur.

The Atheist explanation for creation is that, by the laws of probability, given enough time and innumerable stars, a planet like ours was bound to emerge out of the chaos somewhere in the universe. We know it has occurred at least once, as we are here to tell the tale. Fourteen billion years is considered enough time; and trillions of stars are considered to be enough stars. So, according to this theory, we arrived on this planet through a series of lucky chances, aided, once the first life arrived, by natural selection of those accidental mutations which had the best chance of survival in the conditions at the time. Atheists mostly accept that this algorithm of natural selection, called "the Divine Algorithm" by philosopher Robert Wright, played a part in evolution. The big mystery is still: just how did life first start? There are sound theories as to how this might have happened, but no demonstration yet as to how life could have started spontaneously from the primeval planet.

If there is no God, then how do Atheists explain the eagerness of most humans to believe in one? As mentioned in an earlier chapter, Atheists claim that either there is a gene in our DNA or a meme (an embedded cultural trait) that makes us eager to believe in a God due to its survivability value. People who believed in the same God would be inspired through the common belief of their group to fight for their land and their rights. They would not fear death, as they believed there would be an afterlife. They would not fear the enemy because they believed that God was on their side. Without fear of combat, the group would triumph over others, and live to reproduce offspring with the same traits.

Atheists believe that morality evolved before religiosity as either a gene or a meme because it also had survival value. Morality, or reciprocal altruism, encouraged members of the group to treat each other with respect. This in turn strengthened the solidarity of the group, and hence its ability to fight off invaders and to grow or collect enough food to feed the whole group in times of famine. However, psychologist and philosopher William James speculates that morality and religiosity are not the same, implying that they might have evolved separately.

As to the revelations and miracles set out in the Bible, the Atheist would ask why is it that God has decided to speak only to a chosen few, and not all of us all the time. If he is all-powerful, what does he have to lose by revealing himself to all? Why does he not provide irrefutable evidence of his own existence? Why hide his light under a bushel?

Atheists do not believe in the miracles described in the Bible, nor those claimed to be happening today. Anything contrary to science and common sense is suspect. Magicians have been hoodwinking the public for centuries, but there is always a logical explanation for their magic. For an Atheist, explanations for phenomena must be supported by proven science or at least credible scientific theories subject to peer review. Any observations must be repeatable by others using the scientific method. This tends to cast doubt on reports by individuals of communications with God, as these experiences are not repeatable by others (as they are individualistic in nature, as we have discussed in Chapter 2).

An Atheist believes that only the forces of nature are involved in the creation of the universe and its further evolution, and the advent of life, humans and human intelligence. In this, they are not far removed from the views of Pantheists. The difference being that a Pantheist would refer to nature as God. Whereas, an Atheist would say: why bother to call it God, with all the supernatural characteristics which go along with that word? Why not just simply call it nature? On the other hand, a modern Christian might explain creation by saying that everything the Atheist says about it happening through natural causes is correct, but a God is still necessary to set everything in motion in the first place and to control the outcome!

There are two discontinuities in any natural explanation of the origin of the universe and life: first is the Big Bang;

secondly the first appearance of life. There are compelling theories as to how these could have happened, but no proof. No one has yet produced life from inanimate matter in the laboratory, despite claims from molecular biologists for 50 years that this is just around the corner. The beginning of life on earth must have been a unique event, because the genomes of all living things show such similarities as would point to a single source. If life could arise easily from inanimate matter, multiple sources would be expected, given the 3.5 billion year life of our planet. ("The Society of Genes", 2016, by Itai Yanai and Martin Lercher).

The concluding chapter of this book will start from the assumption held by religious people that a creator God (or an alternate) exists, but that he (or it) worked through the laws of nature and certain natural (divine?) algorithms to create the universe. On that theological basis, an attempt will be made to find the common thread running through all religious experiences and all models for God. For Atheists and those who cannot accept that a thinking God created the universe, there will be an alternative model presented in the Appendix. In a slight departure from the Atheist explanation of the origin of the universe and life, it postulates the existence of some sort of transcendental truth manifest as the potentialities of the universe, based on the laws of science and the initial conditions at the Big Bang, and the existence of a series of natural algorithms, which together increase the degree of complexity in our little part of the universe. This is a bit of a stretch for the Atheists, but they already accept the existence of one natural algorithm: evolution of life by natural selection. I am sure they would be open to accepting other natural algorithms in the chain of creation, should they be discovered by scientists at some time in the future. However, before jumping to conclusions, we must take a look at an idea foreshadowed in previous chapters: that God may be in our minds; or for Atheists, that some people may think it so due to psychological phenomena occurring in their heads, rooted in in the memes or genes originating from our deep past.

Chapter 17

Is God Within Our Minds?

Another model for God, not embraced by the monotheistic religions, is that he exists within our own minds. If so, then is he also present within the structure of living, human DNA, which initiates the development of our brains, and hence minds? Or, would he enter our minds in the womb? If indeed God is present within human DNA then why not the DNA of all life forms down to the primitive, single-cell creatures? This implies that God is synonymous with life. Tolstoy, in his novel "War and Peace" exhorts us to love life, even in adversity, because God is life, and to love life is to love God.

The sacrament of Holy Communion, celebrates the Last Supper, and entails the worshipers taking bread, which Jesus asked them to eat as *"this is my body"* and to drink wine, which Jesus said was his blood, *"which is poured out for many for the forgiveness of sins"* (Mathew 26:26-28). This sacrament could figuratively bring Jesus inside of us, or put us inside Jesus. The latter seems to be the theistically correct interpretation, as it fits with the desire of the faithful to be saved through or in Jesus Christ. *"Do you not know that your bodies are members of Christ"* (1 Corinthians 6:15). Yet, to be in Jesus Christ surely means that he would also be within us! *"It is no longer I who live, but Christ who lives in me"* (Galatians 2:20). But the understanding of traditional Christian theologians is that God is immanent everywhere within the world, but he is separate and distinct from it. So the scriptures are somewhat contradictory as to whether God is in our minds. However, there is support for this concept within Christian Science and the New Thought Religions, in which God is Mind, and we are part of that mind, and thus possess divinity.

A number of biologists and psychologists have proposed that we have a God module in our brains. This postulate is often quoted to explain why we have a natural tendency to believe in God: that it was imprinted in our DNA and in our brains during evolution because it had survivability value. Even without a God module in our brain, Atheists might still say that God is in our imagination, and hence in our minds. They claim that all the stories of the Bible have been made up or at least embellished by mortals. The stories come from their imagination, so it is said, and therefore their minds.

However, leaving skepticism aside, when people report that God has communicated with them, then this message must have come into their minds somehow, which means it must have been received by their brains, which form the platform for their minds. So, even if God does not live within our brains, then it seems he must use the brain as some sort of communications center through which he can relay messages. Yet, those who say they are in contact with God, can sometimes report ecstatic religious experiences, which must involve the emotions and thus the hormones and heart as well. So not all communications from what is perceived to be God come exclusively through the mind it seems. Some must come through the body as well, which, like the brain, is also programmed by our DNA.

First thing we must determine is whether revelations, visions, voices from God or angels, feelings about the presence of God and hallucinations about God or angels or Jesus Christ are real events in people's minds, or are they some psychopathological condition. We are not so much concerned with responses to personal petitions to God, though these be of great importance to the persons receiving them. Rather, we are more concerned with the revelations received by prophets such as Moses, Jesus, Paul, Muhammad, etc., which have changed humanity and history in a fundamental way. If in fact these phenomena are deemed real, then they may well be as real for the individual petitioner as for the prophets: the same mechanism may be operative in each case.

Take Moses for example, before the Ten Commandments and the Torah were revealed to him on Mt Sinai. According to the scriptures he was a leader of his people out of slavery in Egypt, who wanted to keep them on the right moral path. A practical man if ever there was one, and not the kind of person one would expect to have flights of fancy. St. Paul, was a Jew, trained in Greek law, stamping out Christianity for the Roman Government before his conversion on the road to Damascus. Though he was reportedly an epileptic, this may only have served to heighten his sensitivity to a vision of the risen Christ, rather than been the root cause of it. Furthermore, his beautiful sermons and letters, which later formed his Gospel, extending over many years, could all hardly be attributed to epileptic fits. According to Islamic history, Muhammad was an astute businessman before receiving his revelations from Allah through the angel Gabriel, and later became a successful political and military leader. This is hardly the kind of person to have been mentally unhinged.

It is worth examining the Islamic record of Muhammad's revelations and automatic reciting, which may have come from the subconscious sphere of his mind. According to Augustus Clissold in his book "The Prophetic spirit in Genius and Madness", 1870, p 67: *"Muhammad is said to have answered that sometimes he heard a knell as from a bell, and that this had the strongest effect on him, and when the angel went away he had received the revelation. Sometimes again he held converse with the angel, as with a man, so as easily to understand his words. The later authorities however distinguish still other kinds. In the Itgan (103) the following are enumerated: 1, revelations with sound of bell, 2, by inspiration of the Holy Spirit in Muhammad's heart, 3, by Gabriel in human form, 4, by God immediately, either when awake (as in his night journey to heaven) or in dream".*

Automatic and semi-automatic composition was also inspired in Joseph Smith, founder of the Mormon religion, but not so much in Jesus, St Paul and St Augustine. They had revelations as if they had been used as a vehicle or a mouthpiece of a higher power. The implication is that these inspirations may all have come from or through religious experiences possibly arising out of the subconscious minds of the prophets.

Leo Tolstoy, the famous Russian novelist, a task-oriented man if ever there was one, entered into a period of profound depression mid-career, lasting 2 years. He was only able to pull himself out of it by converting to Christianity after he reported a closeness to God. This may well have occurred in his subconscious mind. Many other famous people, and many more not so famous, have reported these mystical conversions. The conscious mind is usually unaware of much that is going on in the subconscious, except for the instance of dreams. As William James asked: *"who is to say there is not an even deeper mind - a religious mind, of which the conscious mind is equally unaware?"*

We can use two criteria to judge whether the prophets' revelations were real. The first is anthropological: to consider whether they have had an effect on the real human world; which undoubtedly they have, in a most remarkable way. The second is scientific. If these revelations were occurring in the minds of the prophets, then they must have been doing so in parallel with electronic and electrochemical events in the neurons of their brains, as neuroscientists are wont to tell us (Jeeves). Such electrical signals are essentially part of the physical world in the brain, and hence are real. Yet, these same electrical events occur in the brain of an author while she is writing fiction. However, fiction is not reality; rather it is an extraction from reality, reconstituted. To determine whether a religious experience is real and not a concoction of fiction, we need to look to see if the religious experience has significantly changed the life of the subject and of others. If it has, then it is different to a fictional event, which usually does not significantly change the life of the author (unless her book is a best-seller and makes her rich and famous) or of others. A delusional person will also have electrical events occurring in his brain during a delusional event. To determine whether a religious experience is delusional or not, we need to look at the subject's behavior in his non-religious life: if it is rational, then the religious experience is real.

So, if God and the angel Gabriel are indeed spiritual beings, as most theologians would maintain, then it seems they have found a way to communicate with the physical world in the brains of the prophets. If the prophets, then why not the brains of some ordinary humans who are sensitized to such messages?

Just how could God be thought to communicate with our brains? The human brain is the most complex organ in the universe, and we are only just starting to unravel its mysteries. Who knows what communication channel has been implanted there over the past million years by evolution, under its own steam or guided by God? If it has been implanted in our brains, it must be also implanted in our DNA, which controls the development of our brains from the moment of conception. It also controls the development of the modus operandi of our brains, i.e. our minds, modified by our experiences in the world. This raises a question central to the theme of this book: *If God's faculty for access to him is in the Torah, the Gospels and the Quran, then why should it not also be in the code within human DNA, which is, after all, part of God's creation?* We know that evolution has encoded our DNA with traits that enhanced our adaptability to challenging human and natural environments. Such traits include willingness to fight against predators and competitors as well as the gifts of language, morality and intelligence to support teamwork. Yet, history has shown a tendency for violence to overshadow morality when times are bad. This could lead to disaster for the human race in times of huge armies and weapons of mass destruction. Maybe God (or whatever assumes the role of God), through evolution, has planted a secret code in our DNA to avert such a catastrophe? It may be accessed more easily by some humans (such as the Prophets) than others; or it may require specific circumstances, including religious training, before it can be expressed

The DNA of all living creatures is like a computer program, crammed with masses of coded instructions to ensure the development and survival of the animal. For readers unfamiliar with genetics and molecular biology, here is a quick lesson. Of the trillion or so of normal cells in the human body, each has a complete copy of the individual's genome (which comprises our DNA) in the nucleus of the cell. There are some 6 billion letters in the code of the individual human genome. This is 1000 times the number of letters in the complete works of William Shakespeare (see "The Society of Genes", by Itai and Lercher, 2016). The text for this code consists of a string of only four letters, repeated over and over again with slight variations. These letter codes are divided into 46 volumes, each one called a chromosome. A chromosome is a giant molecule, consisting of one unbroken double strand of DNA, composed of millions of the four letters strung along it. In reality these letters are chemical bases labelled: A, T, C and G. Just as texts in human language can be divided into paragraphs representing more or less coherent thoughts, so the DNA can be partitioned into discrete fragments of coherent information, called genes. So each DNA double strand contains multiple genes with inherited information capable of being transcribed onto new proteins being synthesized. There are some 20,000 genes in the human genome for manufacturing proteins which are the workhorses and structural components of the human body and brain. The Human Genome Project has confirmed that 82% of our genes are expressed in the brain (Michio Kaku, "The Future of the Mind", 2014)

With so much code in the human genome, if indeed there be a God, why should he not have wanted to leave a faculty for access to him within it? After all, the human being must be his prize creation. The code for such a faculty would be replicated in the cells of our brain and hence find a way into the mind, which is the software operating within the brain. The faculty would then have been available to gifted people, such as Moses, Jesus and Muhammad, facilitating the revelations which they had. This hypothesis will be further explored and substantiated in the next chapter.

If only 75% of religious persons, and none of the irreligious, have religious experiences enabling them to access what they believe to be a God within their minds, then what of those of us who are left out in the cold? How can religious ideas with all their benefits be incorporated in society when only a part of it would seem to be in direct communication with God? The others would need to be won over with a religion which harnesses their energies for the good. If the irreligious become religious, and receive religious training, then there is a 75% chance they will have religious experiences, according to studies quoted in Chapter 2. If we delve back in the past, we see how outsiders were brought into the fold in the Roman Empire and later throughout Medieval Europe. First, in Roman times, Christianity started out as a religion for the oppressed. It offered hope where there was none, love where there was only bitterness, a sense of community in the face of a brutal occupying army. The willingness of Christians to face death rather than give up their God, inspired many converts. Once these converts received religious training many of them would have been sensitized to have religious experiences, i.e. what they believed to be direct communications with God through their minds. Later, once Christianity became the official religion of the Roman Empire in the 4th C, the Roman Church took over the task of winning converts. Since the Church fathers had a monopoly on education and access to the scriptures, often written in classical Latin or Greek beyond the understanding of ordinary folk, this made the task of converting the masses somewhat easier. The educated clergy were held in great esteem by the laity. The scriptures in the Holy Bible, interpreted by the clergy, were deemed the word of God, taking advantage of great reverence for old manuscripts at the time. The Clergy consolidated their power over the people by building breathtaking cathedrals, and introducing ritual, singing, ceremonies and sacraments, which had the effect of bonding religious communities together through the sharing of religious joy and awe. They created social benefits for members, such as alms for the poor. They fostered the belief that they were in direct contact with God, and the laity could communicate with him through them. They offered the prospect of eternal damnation in hell for unbelievers, and eternal life in heaven to believers. They gained political power, and the right to try people for heresy, which carried the death penalty. The Church made saints out of people who had visions or experiences of God, and broadcast these stories far and wide. Kings hijacked the religion, claiming divine right of kingship, thus bolstering their political power and legitimacy. All monarchs and their courts embraced Christianity in Medieval Europe. It was impossible to get a senior posting if you were not a Christian. In short the combined power of the Church and State was wielded in an indoctrination effort on a massive scale.

We see the same forces at work in traditional Muslim countries today. There are huge social advantages in being a practicing Muslim in those countries. In fact, not belonging can bring penalties, often severe. Once in the fold and exposed to religious training, we would expect 75% of them to have religious experiences, based on the percentage in Christian communities as described in Chapter 2.

What then of today in Christianity? The same mechanisms are not available as in the past. Literacy is universal in most countries. People can read their own Bible and just about any other literature they care to take up. However, close-knit religious communities are still able to propagate the belief in God through educating their children as Christians from a very early age. These religious beliefs and values tend to stick, paving the way for the next generation of believers, many of whom would be sensitized to have religious experiences and what they believe to be direct communications from God through their minds. But, the numbers of regular churchgoers continues to shrink every year, especially in Europe. The temptations of the material world are becoming too strong as economic growth and political freedom spread over the face of the earth. Many are happy with the here and now, and think little about the afterlife. The great advances and success of science have made inroads into traditional religious belief, and have called into question many miraculous claims in the Bible. This has led to a credibility gap for Christianity among some of those who cannot claim direct communications with God.

The United States has experienced less shrinkage of churchgoers than has Europe. This is partly due to the rise of less traditional religions there, which offer a form of faith best suited to the inclinations of the parishioners, whether that be confronting sin, in the case of revivalist meetings and traditional Protestantism, to denying sin and concentrating on positive growth, as in the case of modern Protestantism (e.g. Unitarianism), Christian Science, New Thought religions and the Mormons. Church groups form the basis of communities in America much more than they do in Europe. They fulfill social needs as well as personal ones. Also, American pastors are better showmen than their brothers in Europe, making attendance at Church more rewarding. This is carried to extremes with televangelists. Thus, even for the 25% of congregants who report no direct messages from God through their minds, there are still many rewards to be had from being part of a church congregation.

If, as explored in Chapter 15, God is not a thinking God but some Transcendental Truth and teleology, which respectively sets the stage for and steers the evolution of the universe and life, then how could such non-thinking entities reach into in our minds? One explanation is that they must also have played a part in designing our DNA, and hence our brains during evolution. That is, they accomplished what otherwise would have been done by a thinking God. If a non-thinking God can be accessed in our brains, then so too for our minds. This theme will be further developed in the Appendix. But, before that, we need to derive the major conclusions of this book.

Chapter 18

Conclusions

If God's faculty for access to him is in the Torah,
the Gospels and the Quran, then why should it not
also be in the code within human DNA, which is,
after all, part of God's creation?

As described in the preceding chapters, even among the monotheistic religions, God may wear many cloaks, exhibit a variety of behaviors and modus operandi, share his divinity with angels, prophets, saints and popes, possess multiple personalities, promulgate a multitude of laws, and dwell either exclusively in the spirit world or in both the physical and spiritual worlds. There are hundreds of monotheistic religious denominations and sects, only a few of which have been covered in this book, and all have a different concept of God. Those religions which maintain that their God is the one true God must necessarily contend with competing claims from other religions. Even within the one religion, anecdotal evidence from philosophers, psychologists, believers, priests and nuns suggests that the kinds of private beliefs the individual has about her God may be as numerous as the number of adherents to that particular faith. For the sake of order, one is tempted to ask whether or not one common truth or set of truths underlies all religion; whether the one God is beneath the many cloaks he wears.

In previous chapters we have outlined the various models for God held by the main religions, denominations and sects. In particular, we have examined them according to certain important criteria in the hope that we might find some common thread, assuming that there is one. It is worth restating these criteria and the way each religious denomination meets each one. The criteria are as follows.

1. Metaphysics. What alternative reality to the material world exists? Is there a spiritual world or a world of mind separate from the material world?
2. Theology. Is there one God or many? Does he dwell in some alternate reality or the material world or both? Is he interventionist or not?
3. Does God provide an afterlife for the believer?
4. What characteristics does this God possess? Is he a person or an indefinable being? Is he angry or loving or both? Is he optimistic or pessimistic or both?
5. What laws does he promulgate for humans to follow?
6. How do believers communicate with their God? Is it through their minds? Do they have religious experiences during these communications?

In the case of Judaism, 1. A spiritual and material world both exist; 2. One interventionist God exists in one person;

3. God does not provide an afterlife; 4. God is a person. He can be angry and loving, optimistic or pessimistic; 5. God's laws are written into the Torah by divine revelation; 6. Believers communicate with God through prayer or rituals, either privately within their own minds or in a synagogue. Devout Jews pray for many hours of the day, often repeating phrases over and over again, accompanied by rhythmic bowing of the head, which may put them into a kind of religious trance.

For traditional Christianity, 1. A spiritual world and a material world exist side by side. 2. The one interventionist God exists in three persons. All three dwell in the spiritual world, but God the Son spent some time in the material world in human form; 3. God provides an afterlife; 4. God is generally regarded as a person, but some progressive Christians may regard him as an indefinable being. He can be both angry and loving, optimistic or pessimistic; 5. God requires his people to follow the laws laid down in the revealed Bible, as interpreted by the clergy, to a greater or lesser extent: 6. Jesus lived his life as if his ego had completely disappeared under the will of God, exemplifying the absorption of the self within God; In the case of Catholics, they communicate with God through prayer, ritual and singing in their church congregation, achieving communal bonding. Protestants may communicate through prayer privately or sing and pray in a church congregation. Christians report private religious experiences.

For Deism, 1. In the world in which we live there is only one reality, the material world; 2. At the beginning of time and at the birth of the universe a transcendent God existed to set the ball rolling, and thereafter was non-interventionist; 3. The Deist God does not provide an afterlife; 4. He is an indefinable, distant being, neither angry nor loving, optimistic nor pessimistic; 5. He provides only the laws of nature, but allows humans to make their own moral and civil laws; 6. He does not communicate with his followers, who are thus not able to have religious experiences with him.

For Buddhism, 1. There are two realities, the world of consciousness and the material world, of which the first is the most important; 2. There is no God in the formal sense, but meditators often conjure up their own deity or godhead; 3. There is no afterlife, but there is reincarnation in which one's consciousness is inherited from a dead person; 4. In the absence of a God the Buddha is held up as leading the ideal kind of life; 5. Buddhists follow the laws of the right path of the Buddha; 6. Buddhists have spiritual experiences during meditation by extinguishing the boundaries of the self, and thereby entering an alternate reality or altered state of consciousness.

For Islam, 1. In traditional Islam there are two realities, the material world and the spiritual world. Sufi Muslims recognize only one reality, God in the spiritual world; 2. God lives in the spiritual world, but intervenes in the material world, his creation; 3. God provides an afterlife in heaven; 4. God is an indefinable being, but in human terms is given 99 characteristics, including love and anger. The Sufi Muslims regard him as pure love; 5. Traditional Muslims live their lives according to Sharia law, which was devised by the religious scholars, based on the Quran and the life of Muhammad, with much human interpretation since; 6. Muslims communicate with their God through prayer five times a day. Their founder had religious experiences for 22 years when he received the Quran from God. Traditional Muslims believe in submitting the self completely to the will of God. Sufis drown themselves in God.

For Christian Science, 1. There is only one reality, mind, the material world being an illusion; 2. There is one God who is mind, and humans are part of that mind; 3. Mind does not die when the body dies; 4. God is not a being, but the principle of being, at once the law of creation, the substance from which all things are made and the order which harmonizes the cosmos. He is love, good, truth, life, wisdom; 5. Members follow the teachings of Jesus without the dogma and doctrine introduced by the Roman Catholic Church; 6. Adherents appeal through their minds to the mind of God, with which they are conjoined, to heal sickness, and energize their lives.

For Hinduism, 1. There is only one reality, ultimate reality or Brahman (or God if you like), the material world being regarded as an illusion like in a dream; 2. There are many ways to Brahman, through many interventionist gods; 3. Hindu's believe in reincarnation and karma, whereby the good done by a soul in one life determines the quality of the next; 4. Depending on the personality of the believer, God can be a transcendent being centered on the believer, or can be a personal God like the Christian God; 5. The law of karma ensures that Hindus lead a good life in this world; 6. Hindus seek to reach God through meditation and yoga, enabling them to reach deep into their minds to move from the small, limited self to the wider sphere of human existence and ultimately to God.

For Scientology, 1. Reality is composed of spirit rather than matter; 2. Scientologists believe in ultimate reality rather than a creator God, humans in their spiritual form being the creators of the universe; 3. Spiritual humans are reborn into the physical world with each generation, and return to the spiritual world on the death of the human body they inhabited; 4. There is a cosmic source or life force in place of a God, and humans are the individualized expression of this; 5. By a process of purification from the temptations of the material world, humans may eventually become gods and live to infinity; 6. Humans communicate with their spiritual selves through their minds by intense study and ritual, similar to meditation in eastern religions.

For Mormonism, 1. The material world is more important than the spiritual world; 2. There is one God who rules over a council of gods; 3. There is an afterlife in the future Kingdom of God, which will be on earth, in Utah; 4. God is a person, who once lived in material form; 5. God's laws are as laid down in the Bible and the writings of Joseph Smith and his successors; 6. Members of the church communicate with their God through their minds by intense study and rituals, as in eastern religions.

For Taoism, 1. This religion is concerned with the material world. There is a transcendent sense of the Tao, the ordering principle behind all life, and an immanent sense, the driving power behind all nature; 2. There is no personal God in the original form of Taoism, rather there is ultimate reality; 3. There is no afterlife, only union with nature; 4. The Tao is a principle of being; 5. Taoism has a bible, the Tao Te Ching, which if followed will revitalize the self; 6. Taoists communicate with the Tao through their minds, suppressing the ego and approaching a state of peace into which the energy of the Tao can flow.

By comparing the above, we see that there is little commonality within the first five criteria. There is no shared concept of reality or metaphysics across the board; there is no common theology; there is no consistent promise of an afterlife; there is no common model for God; there is no common set of divine laws. It is with the sixth criteria that we see much commonality. What is common to all religions (except for Deism) is a desire for expanding the limited concept of the self into the wider sphere of human existence and ultimately to God. This is achieved by delving deep into the mind through meditation, intense concentration, yoga, and prayer, trances produced by rhythmic repetitive behavior such as chanting, dancing, communal singing and rituals, the outcomes of which are called religious experiences.

On a social level, certainly all religions build cohesion, and stress the need for love and a moral and ethical code within human communities to ensure peace and harmony. Most believers enjoy the poetry of the group singing, chanting, rituals and celebrations associated with worship. However, as mentioned above, religion goes even deeper, at a personal level. Psychologist and philosopher William James states in his classic 1902 book "Varieties of Religious Experience" that: *"religious belief consists of the belief that there is an unseen order, and that our supreme good lies in harmoniously adjusting ourselves thereto."* James claims that beliefs more elaborate than that constitute "over-belief" developed for, embraced by, and specific to, every one of the various religions and denominations. In other words the various religions may be metaphorical expressions of some deeper reality. James' definition seems a good starting point in our search for a common thread in the models for God.

The Common Thread - A Faculty in the Mind to Access a God

To help in our search, the comparative study of the various religions has left an important clue. Many religious followers of Hinduism, Buddhism, Scientology, Taoism and Sufi Islam, use meditative techniques and rituals to experience the divine. This involves delving into the deeper recesses of the mind, blurring the boundaries of the limited self, thereby opening the mind up to alternate realities and even God. Christian Scientists and New Thought religions go one step further and consider their minds to be part of the mind of God. Sufi Muslims drown themselves in God during trances. Traditional Muslims within their minds submit themselves to the will of God. Mainstream Christians give God control over their lives. Within Christianity and Islam, the prophets experienced revelations from God through their minds. Furthermore, 75 percent of Christian believers report religious experiences within their minds of a highly individualistic nature. These clues all point to a conclusion that is somewhat paradoxical: the common thread running through all models for God is an innate faculty within the individual human mind enabling the extension of the boundaries of the limited self in order to reach out to a God. This customized approach to what is believed to be God is what produced the great variety of religious experiences among founders of the many religions and their followers. This faculty provides a gateway into the wider sphere of human existence and even into the supernatural, through which the individual may find her God, whomever or whatever he may be. It is postulated that this faculty is innate within all humans; but only 75% are able to access it by being sensitized culturally through their religious training, given their nature and life circumstances. This faculty provides someone to pray to, receive messages from, or to move beyond the self and the material world with. Such a definition allows us to include other religions such as Hinduism, which are not strictly monotheistic. Rather than finding God within their minds, Hindus and Buddhists find ultimate reality or nirvana. I leave it up to the reader to decide whether she thinks these religious/spiritual experiences are real. They are certainly real to the people who are having them. I say that this God is accessed within the mind, because that is where the believer, in private, experiences God. If believers did not have these personal experiences of God, then organized religion would quickly collapse. Yet, without the template of beliefs provided by organized religion, individuals would have no religious experiences. One cannot exist without the other. The existence of religious training is a necessary (but not sufficient) trigger for access to what individuals believe to be a God in the mind, although without that training, some may still have spiritual experiences of a non-religious kind. Furthermore, the specific nature of these religious experiences, as reported by the believer, are conditioned by the religious faith, denomination and sect in which he has been raised and to which he belongs; and there are hundreds of them. A Christian may feel the presence of Jesus; whereas a Muslim will feel the presence of Allah. What's more, the concept of God which the individual believer carries in her mind will depend on her own personality, character, mood, beliefs and values, for example whether she is a healthy-minded person or a sick-soul that needs saving. Given the unique nature of every individual, it is possible that there could be as many concepts of God as there are believers on the face of the earth. Why should a God wish it so? Wouldn't it be simpler if he appeared before us all in public so that we may all have the same standardized image of him? However, that is not to be. It is not to be because what is believed to be God is accessed in the minds of those so sensitized, and is thus subject to individualistic perception, which thereby makes him more aligned with the believer, and thus more approachable.

It is postulated that all humans possess a faculty in their minds to access religious experience of what is believed to be a God, but only about 75% get to access this faculty during their lives. Substantiation of this hypothesis will be provided shortly. Some significant fraction of humans never experience this God, or experience him only when under severe stress such as when approaching death. This fraction of the population would include up to 25% or so of religious persons plus all non-believers. The combination of their own nature, their life experiences, the surrounding culture and their religious training, if any, would not have been sufficient to enable access to what is believed to be a God in the mind.

The next question is this: if these experiences of a God are only in the mind, then are they real? Yes, they are real for two reasons. The first is the effect that they have on the real world. Undoubtedly these experiences in the form of conversions etc. have a direct effect on the individual's life thereafter. He may change his church, his worshiping habits and his life choices. When important prophets, such as Moses, Jesus, Paul and Muhammad, have had these experiences in the form of revelations, they have changed the course of history in fundamental ways and established master models for God. Secondly, the experiences are real because neuroscience tells us that anything going on in the mind is mirrored by electrical and electrochemical events in the brain; and such events are of the physical world, and are undoubtedly real. In fact brain imaging experiments have shown activity in the temporal lobe of the cerebral cortex in the brain (where concepts are put together) in believers who reported having religious experiences at the time (Jeeves). The pre-frontal lobe of the cortex, the seat of the will, also shows activity during meditation, as does the parietal lobe, the orientation area (Newberg et al). Yet, similar electrical events must occur somewhere in the brain of an author while she is writing fiction; and fiction is not reality; rather it is an extraction from reality, reconstituted. To determine whether a religious experience is real and not a concoction of fiction, we need to look to see if the religious experience has significantly and permanently changed the life of the subject and others. If it has, then it is different to a fictional event, which usually does not so change the life of the author (unless her book is a best-seller and makes her rich and famous), or of others. A delusional person will also have electrical events occurring in the brain during a delusional experience. To tell whether or not a religious experience is real or a delusion, we need to look at the behavior of the subject in his or her non-religious life: if it is rational, then the religious experience is real.

Given that these experiences are deemed real in a pragmatic way, just what makes religious people believe that they are accessing God within their minds? This God is accessible in ways that are tailored to the individual concerned. There are of course supernatural explanations, but before we go there we should explore possible natural processes behind the belief that a God is being accessed in the mind, even if some may stretch scientific understanding beyond where it currently stands. The hypothesis is that there is a code for religiosity, usually manifest as the felt presence of a God in the mind, within human DNA, put there when our ancestors first evolved on the planet in what we now know as human form. This code finds its way into our minds through the development of the brain from the embryo, which is controlled by our DNA. For a general description of the code within the human genome and DNA, the reader is referred to the previous chapter. As to how this code was put there, or who put it there, we will come to later. We hypothesize further that this code has an influence on our DNA in its design of our brains, including the way they operate, and this design feature sits there latently. Then something in the individual's personal nature, life experiences, environment and religious training activates this feature and creates this experience of a God within her mind. The believer perceives this experience as meaningful, as a God, not some indecipherable code or electrons running through the neuronal circuits of the brain. This is the same as when someone receives an email on their computer or smart phone. They receive meaning, not code or movements of electrons. But the software program in their device does see code, and its circuitry does see electrons moving. In summary, it is hypothesized that the faculty enabling religious people to believe they are accessing a God inside their minds arises from a design of the brain by the DNA, including its modus operandi. This faculty was put in place during much earlier times in our evolution, perhaps 100,000 years ago before humans as we know them first emerged from Africa.

How can this hypothesis be substantiated? What is the scientific evidence from genetics and neuroscience? As mentioned earlier, there are about 20,000 genes in the human genome, and researchers have found about 82% of them to be expressed in the brain. One gene, VMAT2, has been found by a research team at Harvard (Hamer) to have a tiny (1%) influence on the trait of "self-transcendence", a neutral measure of spirituality. Yet, no gene has yet been found which contains the code enabling access to religious experiences of a God within the human mind. This is perhaps not surprising in these early days of molecular biology. That is because genes, or combinations of genes, have multiple roles within the human body and brain (Yanai). Thus a gene already identified as having a role unrelated to religious experience arguably may still be involved in some way in emplacing a latent access to what is believed to be a God in the mind. This is likely to be a multi-gene arrangement, given the complexity of religious experiences, and thus difficult to discover, assuming it exists. Even if a gene or group of genes is suspected of playing such a role, it will be all but impossible to prove from clinical evidence. This would involve finding someone lacking these genes through some fault of nature, indoctrinating her with religion, and then asking her if she subsequently has religious experiences. If she does not, then chances are that the right genes have been found. The experiment would need to be repeated with new subjects to demonstrate that it was statistically significant. Such a set of experiments would be ethically questionable, and therefore may never be performed.

Recent studies (2012) in the US, Australia and the UK of identical twins raised in different households have shown that genetic factors account for 40-50% of religiosity, assessed by answers to questions which measure spirituality independent of the formal theology of the religious institution, if any, to which the subject belonged (Spector). These questions were designed to measure self-forgetfulness, transpersonal identification and mysticism. A typical question was: "I believe that all life depends on some spiritual order or power that cannot be completely explained" – true or false? Another study was performed in 2013 on 2,237 Danish same-sex, identical and fraternal twins born 1970-1989 who were sent a web-based survey. It was found that personal religiousness, such as praying to God, believing in God, and finding strength and comfort in religion, were more influenced by genetic factors than were social forms of religiousness such as church attendance (Hvidtjorn et al). The conclusion that can be drawn from these studies is that susceptibility to spirituality seems to be influenced by genetics, but the form that it takes is culturally determined. This conclusion inferentially supports the hypothesis presented here that the code for access to religious experience of what is believed to be a God within the mind is in the genes, but the form that such a God takes is culturally determined.

There are two ways to interpret the twin studies. One way, proposed by Hamer, is that the propensity to have religious/spiritual experiences is genetically determined, but varies considerably from one person to another. Another way, proposed here, is that everyone has a faculty in their brains enabling religious/spiritual experiences in their minds, which is genetically determined, but only certain persons are able to access that faculty. Such persons would have the nature, life experiences and religious training sufficient to do so. In other words, religiosity is analogous to language: every human has the innate faculty, but only those exposed to a specific language will learn to speak; and their speech will reflect the culture in which they are raised; and of those so exposed some will make greater use of the faculty than others due to their overall mental and emotional abilities.

What then is the neuroscientific evidence for a design of the human brain and its operating system that would produce a latent access to what is believed to be a God in the mind? Certainly brain imaging has found localized activity in the temporal lobe of the brain in believers who reported having religious experiences at the time (Jeeves). However, to prove the hypothesis that this is due to the faculty for religious experience being present in the brain, researchers would need to stimulate this region of the brain in a conscious believer, and ask the subject whether he has a religious experience at the time. If he did, the right spot would have been found. Chances are, however, that stimulation of just the temporal lobe would fail to produce a religious experience anyway. That is because religious experiences doubtless involve the pre-frontal and parietal lobes as well, along with the emotions through the participation of the older limbic system of the brain, such as the amygdala, hypothalamus and hippocampus. These are in contact with the hormonal system, the heart and the sympathetic and parasympathetic nervous systems in the rest of the body (Newberg et al). Further, such an experiment could ethically only be carried out if the brain had been laid open for unrelated medical reasons. Even then, the practical difficulties in such an experiment seem insurmountable. Needless to say, this experiment has not been performed and is unlikely to be so. Furthermore, experimenters do not have the luxury of using laboratory animals as analogues for human behavior in this instance because, as far as we know, animals do not have religious experience, and even if they did there is no way they could tell us about it.

A word of caution: even if a faculty exists enabling access to what is believed to be a God in the mind this does not prove that God exists. It may only have been an accident of evolution. However, if God does exist, then what better way could he have found to communicate with his followers at a personal level?

Given the limited availability of direct scientific evidence, it is necessary to use supplementary indirect evidence from genetics, evolutionary biology, neuroscience, psychology, anthropology and logic to substantiate our hypotheses. First, we know from the migratory habits of birds, salmon and whales that they are born with some innate map which enables them to find their way back to the same place every year over thousands of miles of ocean. While humans do not have these skills, it does not disqualify them from having evolved some other innate abilities in their brains that may have had survivability benefits for them. The evolutionary mechanism is there for this. For example, as Plato pointed out 2,500 years ago, the ability to understand the meaning of the concepts of "equal to", or "greater than" or "less than" is in the human at birth, and not learned subsequent to it. What's more, babies at birth instinctively know how to suckle at their mother's breast. These skills are innate. Furthermore, anthropologists hold that human religious ritual, which people enjoy, goes back to animal ritual, which is innate. Thus, there is no reason, from an evolutionary biological point of view, why humans could not be born with an innate faculty for experiencing what they believe to be a God in the mind if it were to have bestowed adaptive benefits during evolution, enabling the possessor of that faculty a greater chance of living long enough to reproduce.

There is an argument mounted by some anthropologists that, during evolution, religiosity has ridden on the backs of other possibly inherited traits, such as morality, which do have survivability benefits (by forging group cohesion); that it is serendipity which has given us religion, just like it has given us the ability to compose and appreciate music and do calculus, which, on the face of it, also do not seem to have had survivability benefits. Yet, a closer inspection of these skills shows otherwise. Linguists maintain that singing evolved before speech in the evolution of language (Yunai); and the evolution of the ability to mentally compute the direction and trajectory of a spear thrown towards prey or an enemy had huge survivability benefits. Thus there are precedents for a faculty like religiosity to have been naturally selected during evolution, if it had survivability benefits, and not to have been the result of serendipity.

Was religiosity an outgrowth of morality? Perhaps not. William James has maintained that religion and morality are not the same. James writes that: *"many non-churchgoers claim that they can lead moral lives without religion. But it is not the same. The difference between morality and religion is that morality requires effort and tends to vanish when circumstances deteriorate"* (such as happened during the two world wars). *"On the other hand, religion provides peace of mind even when times are bad. It provides an additional enchantment over and above the feeling of purely moral good. It is solemn and serious. The abandonment of self-responsibility and allowing God to take over seems to be the fundamental act in specifically religious, as distinguished from moral, practice."* So, there could be a code in the human genome which creates a faculty in the brain giving access to religious experiences, separate from a code for morality; that is, the two of them could have played different roles during evolution. Morality has been observed in chimps and monkeys, and may have been inherited by them and by us from our common ancestor. Religiosity is not observed in chimps and monkeys. It may have had its own unique survivability benefit to offer humankind, and thus have evolved through a different path than morality, as outlined in Chapter 2. In brief, members of a tribe with religious beliefs about a life after death, bolstered by religious experiences of a spirit world during induced trance-like states, would have had the reassurance that their spirits would protect them in battle. These beliefs would have caused them to lose their fear of failure and death, thereby bestowing huge benefits during inter-tribal wars which were rife 50,000 years ago. The victorious religious tribe would have lived to propagate its religious genes, and the irreligious tribes would have been wiped out.

The next question is whether religiosity is in the genes or the memes? Was it acquired during evolution, or passed down through culture? Richard Dawkins claims the latter. Let us take a look at this claim. The human race emerged out of Africa some 50,000 years ago, and migrated from there to distant parts of the globe over the next 40,000 years or so. Analysis of human DNA shows that all humans had the same genetic origin (Yunai). But could one say that they had the same cultural origins? How much of the early African culture could have survived 40,000 years of tribal wars and migration to regions of the world with very different climates to Africa? Probably very little; and so it is unlikely to have been the source of universal religiosity. For example, by 2,500 BC, humans from different parts of the world all differed in their spoken tongues, which was obviously culturally determined; but what they all had in common was the *faculty* of language itself, which is genetically determined, and probably came from humans who originally migrated out of Africa. By 2,500 BC humans also followed a multitude of different religions, the essentials of which were culturally determined, but without exception they all had *some kind* of primitive religion; and the inference is that this religiosity must likewise have been innate; that is genetically determined, as was the faculty of language. According to this argument, genetics determines religiosity; culture determines what kind of religion.

While religious practice and training are obviously passed on to succeeding generations through the culture in which every child is embedded, there is a part of religiosity which cannot be so transmitted. The mental *faculty* enabling 75% of practicing Christians to have religious experiences, like those described in Chapter 2, cannot be sheeted home to culture alone. The same applies to experiences that have been reported by Islamic Sufis, Hindus, Buddhists and other meditative religions described elsewhere in this book. While the template for such experiences, and even the technique for summoning them, are determined by the religion to which the believers belong, the *capability* of the brain to host such experiences must arguably be innate. So also would be the wiring of the brain that bestows such a capability. It is not possible for this wiring to be passed on culturally in humans over the age in which religious indoctrination usually begins. Admittedly, even the adult brain does exhibit some plasticity arising out of experience and learning, but this is usually confined to accumulating memory and establishing new connections to accomplish the same task in a shorter time. This plasticity does not enable the brain to accomplish tasks which are beyond its innate capability (Bear). Analogously, the *potential* to excel at mathematics, music or art is known to be determined by the genes, although cultural influences can develop and enhance this potential. Surely, this is so also for any potential for religiosity which might arise from an innate faculty within the human brain.

Anthropologists tell us that religion arose out of belief in spirits by primitive man who was hard wired by evolution to look for agents in the environment, such as other men, animals or phenomena, as causes for his condition. If no agent could be discerned, then he came to believe in spirits who were invisible to the real world but had an effect upon it. This constituted a pre-scientific explanation for a hostile and capricious world. Later, belief in spirits was elaborated and formalized into religions of various kinds. But something is missing from this explanation of the origin of spirit belief. What faculty in the mind of early man enabled him to make this quantum leap of faith; to use his imagination in this way? Why would he seek an explanation outside the real world which he perceived with his senses and which he knew so well, unless he had an innate predilection to do so? As to where he got this predilection, it came through natural selection during the hunter-gatherer period between 200,000 and 15,000 years ago, as described above and in Chapter 2, during a period when using his imagination gave him a huge survivability advantage. Indeed, why do children believe in ghosts, even today? Why are they ready to believe in mind readers and magicians? There must be a faculty within the brain and its operating system which makes this possible. Then, why not a faculty in the brain for experiencing what is believed to be spirits or a God in the mind?

If such a faculty did indeed get into the human brain through the human genome, then it must have been adaptive during evolution for it to have been naturally selected. On the face of it, participation in time-consuming religious rituals for no material gain would seem to be costly to survival, and hence be non-adaptive. We may then ask what survivability benefits were bestowed by belief in spirits. There are a few, although it is hard to put ourselves in the footsteps of early humans living 15,000-200,000 years ago, when most human evolution from our pre-human ancestors occurred. A scenario is described in Chapter 2 as to how some early humans came to believe in a spirit world. Firstly, they saw living people in their dreams who had already died, giving them the idea that these people were alive in another world. Then an individual was born with a mutation in the gene associated with the neurobiological machinery controlling sexual activity. This gene enabled him to experience ecstasy during altered states of consciousness similar to sexual ecstasy. He discovered he could induce altered states by going into a trance brought on by rhythmic chanting, singing and dancing or the taking of hallucinatory drugs from certain plants. These altered states made him feel as if he was in the spirit world along with the people in his dreams. He convinced others in his tribe that a spirit world existed in which they could all experience a life after death. As explained in the discussion of morality and religiosity above, this gave the tribe a huge advantage in inter-tribal warfare and led to the ecstatic trance-inducing gene spreading through the successful tribe and being reproduced in the next generation, while the members of the other tribes, who did not possess the gene, were wiped out in the wars.

A second possible mode of natural selection is that belief in spirits may have been the beginning of human innovation. If a cause for a phenomenon could not be found in the natural world, then humans may have used their imaginations to search their minds for some other cause. They had to be innovative, so they came up with spirits. They then looked for some forms of human behavior which might have improved their condition, and might have assuaged the spirits. Most of the time they got it wrong (by sacrificing their children, for example), but in a few cases they got it right. Though grounded in superstition, this may have been the beginning of the empirical pre-scientific method. If the procedure were repeated many times, without producing the desired result, then, either the tribe died out (through attrition, for example), fired its witch doctor, or tried something else to assuage the spirits (clearing a ceremonial circle around the village, which just happened to act as a fire break, for example). In this way, humans may have stumbled empirically across the real natural reason for their condition. The tribe that eventually got it right would have survived to live another day, and to reproduce; and its associated religion would have been adaptive for evolution. The empirical method is, after all, the way the early Chinese discovered herbal medicine. Medicine-men in hunter-gatherer societies often invoked the spirits. Where they were also successful in finding herbal cures, this success may have been attributed by their patients to religious practices, thus making religion adaptive, indirectly, for evolution, due to the success of the medicinal herbs in prolonging life of believers sufficient for reproduction to occur.

Other evidence against purely cultural transmission of religiosity is from the effects of hallucinatory drugs.

These are known to cause experiences similar to religious experiences, although not necessarily of a religious nature. This is because drugs cause chemical and physical changes in the brain circuits, which take them outside normal operating conditions (Bear). That is, the behavior changes are attributed to actual physical and chemical changes in the brain. Exposure to any surrounding culture does not do this (except in the case of mental illness induced by anxiety or depression), and therefore, by analogy, such cultural exposure is also unlikely to enable religious experiences, which resemble altered states produced by drugs, (although cultural exposure can affect the type of experience).

In studies described in Chapter 2, non-religious people do report having, spiritual experiences during meditation, the credit for which cannot be laid at the feet of religious cultural indoctrination. The implication is that the predilection to have spiritual/religious experiences may be innate and not culturally determined.

Religious experiences are usually of the emotions as well as the mind. James speaks of religious fear, joy and love. Singing hymns in unison is an emotional experience for Christians. Islamic terrorism is often associated with religious anger, which is an emotion. Most people consider the emotions as being often outside the control of the cognitive mind. They spring up from deep within us. Generally, they are believed to be innate rather than learned. Although it is possible to *learn* what is cause for fear or joy or love or anger, the *feeling itself* is considered part of the person's innate nature. Thus there is strong support for the thesis that emotional religious experiences are likewise innate, but the circumstances that trigger them are learned. There is support for this thesis from neuroscience. The emotions tend to spring from the older parts of the brain such as the hypothalamus and amygdala, which arose very early in our evolution, and which we share with our animal cousins. Though intimately linked through many cross-connections to the cerebral cortex in humans, which is also involved in human emotion, it is the hypothalamus and amygdala which are in direct contact with the pituitary gland and the hormonal system and the autonomous nervous system that produce the raw (animal) emotions in the body. The roles played by these organs during emotional experience and their interconnections are considered innate. The hypothalamus and the amygdala are not the locations where cultural learning takes place. This evidence implies that emotional religious experiences may likewise arise from something innate within the brain.

Finally, if there be no innate connection through the human body and brain with what the faithful believe to be their God, then we are left with what the religions now claim: that the connection is spiritual through some unknown channel.

Where in The Brain Does This Faculty Reside?

It would be a mistake, I feel, to try to find the specific location in the brain of this faculty for accessing what is believed to be a God within the mind. Such would be the so-called "God spot" mentioned by some researchers reporting in popular journals. Certainly, as we have already seen, brain imaging has found localized activity in the temporal lobe of the brain (Jeeves) and the pre-frontal and parietal lobes (Newberg et al) in believers who reported having religious experiences at the time. However, this may only be the tip of the iceberg. The brain operates in a holistic way, pulling in help from many parts through its multiple cross-connections with the emotional seat of the brain in the limbic system comprising the amygdala, hypothalamus and hippocampus. This holistic paradigm is likely to apply especially to complex activity such as religious experiences, which have emotional as well as cerebral content. Rather than in a so-called God-spot in the brain, it is more likely that this faculty is activated in the modus operandi (i.e. the mind) within the brain by specific stimuli. The mind here is analogous to, but not the same as, the software in a computer. These stimuli could be environmental conditions inside and outside the body, religious training and attitudes, the mood, nature and values of the subject, etc. William James speculated in 1902 that this may take place in the sub-conscious mind or even in a part of the mind beyond the subconscious – the religious mind. At the time however there was little understanding of the neurological basis of the sub-conscious, let alone any religious region beyond it. The situation is much the same today. Brain imaging techniques do not tell us whether or not the activity measured during religious experiences is in the sub-conscious mind. This activity takes place in the same brain location as conscious experience.

Sigmund Freud was the father of the sub-conscious. He held that belief in God was a sub-conscious yearning for one's biological father. However, this seems too simplistic an explanation for the wide variety of religious experiences reported. Whatever their location in the brain, they take the form of revelations, conversions, feelings of the presence of God, trances, mystical experiences, visions, voices, guiding impressions, rapture, "openings", automatic writing and speaking (speaking in tongues), dreams or hallucinations. Their significance for humankind is that the faculty providing access through them to what is believed to be a God may enable an appeal directly to human intelligence and compassion to override the brutal characteristics we have inherited from evolution and survival of the fittest. The faculty to communicate with what is believed to be a God through religious experiences is possessed by some but not others, as is the case for mathematical, sporting and musical ability. Those of us who cannot access the faculty, have the option of receiving the message secondhand, as we do for Mozart's music, which we could say was also inspired by God.

The Creator God

So, if there is a code to access what is believed to be a God in the mind, did a creator God put it into the human genome 15,000 to 200,000 years ago, when our human ancestors were undergoing evolution, and why? What was its purpose? A Theist, assuming he would even countenance such an idea, might say that the God who created the universe put it there. He might argue that the creator God so loved his people that he wanted to provide an avenue for each believer to experience her own private God tailored to her distinctive nature. That way, millions of private gods could emanate from the one creator God. Then we could explain the plethora of models for God among the many religions and among individuals within each and every one of those religions. Our hypothetical Theist could argue that the creator God wished to work his wonders through the laws of nature in this way, as he had with the motions of the heavenly bodies and evolution of the species.

By using a private God as his representative within the mind of every believer, a creator God thereby could, arguably, release himself from the task of simultaneously having a dialogue with 3 billion believers on the planet, not to mention keeping an eye on the trillions of stars in the universe – no mean feat, even for a God. A channel is thereby provided for each believer to connect in her own way with what she believes to be the creator God through the faculty in her mind that she has inherited via her distant ancestors.

OK, for the sake of argument, let's assume that this scheme is correct. That being so, the question arises as to just how such a creator God would use the laws and algorithms of nature to achieve this goal of putting this code inside the human genome. For those interested in the mechanism of how this might be done, I refer them to Chapter 2 and the Appendix. For those who are unable to accept a sentient creator God, then the same mechanism, as described in the Appendix, would apply, only with the creator God replaced with whatever achieves the same purpose.

So, to pursue the line of reasoning a little further, the creator God, assuming he exists, may have been responsible, through evolution, for placing this faculty in the brain, not only of ordinary persons, but also of great prophets such as Moses, Jesus and Muhammed. This faculty could have found fertile ground within the minds of unusually gifted individuals, living in extraordinary times and exposed to challenging conditions; and so could have been accessed to produce the revelations that it did. These revelations have shown us another way forward rather than survival of the fittest, which has taken us thus far, but is not suited to a world of massed armies, let alone weapons of mass destruction. The revelations have fundamentally changed the course of human history.

Since Muhammad's message was to bring the God of the Jews and Christians to the Arab world, then this creator God, should he exist, would seem to be one and the same God in all three faiths. That being so, this creator God must necessarily have placed the code for this faculty within the DNA of the ancestors of Muslims as well as Christians, for Muslims and Christians all have the same generic human DNA. This could also be said for Hindus, Buddhists and members of the cults within Islam and the plethora of denominations within Christianity. They must all have the same code within their DNA which is manifest in access within their minds to what is believed to be a God distinctive to each branch of the faiths, and also to the nature, life experiences, circumstances and culture of the individual.

Theological Questions

So, to summarize, it is proposed that the common thread running through all religions is the existence of a faculty enabling access to what is believed to be a God in the mind of the individual, derived from code in the human genome, emplaced there 15,000 -200,000 years ago, during which our ancestors evolved after having acquired human form. This faculty in the mind is the basis of religious experiences by believers, which in turn underpin institutional religion of all kinds, certainly all monotheistic religions. All the colorful religious stories and theologies woven by the various religions into a rich tapestry with this common thread constitute what William James calls "over-belief". It is the metaphorical gilding of the lily. The stories range in color and texture from the basic Deism to the full gamut of biblical stories, prayers, hymns, relics, rituals, ceremonies, creeds, theologies, saints and sacraments of the Roman Catholic Church. These so-called "over-beliefs", which in turn are both necessary for, and affect the nature of, religious experiences, have gained traction in the minds and hearts of believers due to their tremendous human appeal. Many of them are outlined in the preceding chapters of this book.

On the other hand, the bare-bones atheist philosophy is that the propensity to believe in a deity and to have associated religious experiences comes from cultural memes or a part of the brain which has been hard-wired by evolution for a non-religious purpose. It got there either because it was culturally adaptive and had survivability benefits or it hitch-hiked on an inherited trait, such as morality, which did. The Atheist would argue that this propensity to believe in a God has passed its use-by date in the modern world. Furthermore, the Atheist believes the laws of physics are all that is required to ultimately explain the origin and evolution of the universe and human life. There is no need of a creator God, nor any substitute, to hold the secrets of existence and drive things along; but the implication is that we arrived here largely by chance, although once life began the algorithm of natural selection did play a determining role.

The Atheist would argue that man's innate morality is sufficient to steer him through the shoals that lie ahead, and that religion can be safely dumped overboard. Yet, morality without religion seems not enough. During the 75 years of communist rule of the Soviet Union religion was forbidden, or at least discouraged. Society was steered by the morality of communism, such as collective ownership of the means of production, equal distribution of wealth according to need and subjection of the individual's needs to the needs of the communist society. The system was an abysmal failure, and brought out the worst in human beings, such as envy, hoarding, theft, free-loading and laziness, in which neighbors and even family members were reported to authorities for minor infractions of the communist party rules of conduct. What's more the shocking failure of morality during the Second World War by Nazi Germany towards the Jews and other races and by the military Government of Japan towards the Chinese and captured prisoners of war from Britain and Australia can possibly be sheeted home to the decline of religion in the first half of the 20th C in those countries.

As outlined in Chapter 2, religiosity, as distinct from morality, may have become innate in early man more than 50,000 years ago through the benefits it bestowed during inter-tribal war, which was rife in those times. However, it would be an ironic twist of fate for us to use this innate faculty, given how it has been acquired, to create peace. This could be done by enabling individuals to extend the boundaries of the self to the wider sphere of human existence comprising the whole world, and not just the tribal in-group. In that way it may be possible to overcome the law of survival of the fittest, which is also in our genes and which has led to so much violence over the millennia.

For the Theist, the God who is accessed within the mind and the God who created the universe and man are the one God. While a traditional Christian may believe the biblical story that this God made the universe and man in six days about 6,000 years ago, most modern Christians accept that this process was spread over 14 billion years, starting with the Big Bang. They are not worried that God waited so long before creating man within the last 200,000 years. After all, what is 14 billion years to a timeless God? Just the blinking of an eye!

However, in the hypothesis presented here, the faculty for access to what is believed to be a God in the mind would only be as old as the human brain and human DNA, which evolved over the past 200,000 years or so, and thus obviously would not have existed 14 billion years ago when the universe was first created. To create the universe required a creator God or some other first cause. The concept of a faculty providing access to a God being emplaced much later in the human mind by a creator God is not in principle alien to Christianity. After all, Jesus was supposedly placed among the people of the earth by God the Father to provide access to him only 2,000 years ago!

Is the idea of a faculty enabling access in the mind to

what is believed to be a God a satisfactory belief system compared with say traditional Christianity? The answer is that it may underlay traditional Christianity (and other religions) in a number of respects. It does provide access to what is believed to be a personal God, as a kind of father figure, tailored to the believer's own personality who will love her and to whom she can look up to, seek help from, be inspired by, and confide in. Through inspiration by this God she can make her own way in the world using her wits and in co-operation with her brothers and sisters on the planet. This is arguably a faculty with which we are endowed, which many can access with the right religious training. If used in a narrow, bigoted way, it can lead to inhuman outcomes, as experienced during the crusades, the religious wars in Europe and present-day Islamic terrorism. If used in a way inclusive of the whole world it may help to save humankind from destroying itself through unmitigated self-interest and violence.

Appendix

God in the Mind

Using the laws and algorithms of nature, how could a creator God, if he exists, have placed a faculty enabling access within the human mind to what is believed to be a God, and a code for this in the human genome? Could it have been done using the natural algorithm involved in natural selection, i.e. evolution? That could have happened if the existence of such a faculty within the mind had conferred a survivability advantage. If so, this would be something altogether unusual, because most of the adaptive traits acquired during evolution are such as to ensure that the individual survives in an environment where he is in competition with other humans and animals under challenging environmental conditions. Thus, intelligence, fortitude, strength, teamwork and willingness to kill in defense of one's property or even to take over the property of others, would have been selected. These are strange bedfellows indeed with today's religious values of compassion and love, but not with the religious values of our hunter-gatherer ancestors 50,000 years ago when inter-tribal war was rife. At that time, there were survivability benefits from a common religion within the tribe manifest as esprit de corps and loss of the fear of death in battle. Thus competitive violence and religious traits could have co-evolved. When the very survival of the tribe was at stake, the natural (and adaptive) fear of death would have been overridden in battle by belief in an afterlife, giving a huge advantage to the religious tribe over its irreligious opponent. The details of how this could have happened are given in Chapter 2.

A Series of Natural Algorithms – a Teleology

If a putative creator God used the laws of nature to achieve the creation, then he would have needed to make use of a series of natural algorithms to drive the process forward. Evolution by natural selection is the best known natural algorithm. A natural algorithm is a process that by autonomous repetitive actions produces a solution or outcome, i.e. even without a controller such as a human or a God. Other natural algorithms in the chain of creation could conceivably include the repetitive production of the life-giving element carbon at the center of giant stars and the scattering of this carbon through the universe when those stars explode in a supernova. As an aside, non-natural, as opposed to natural, algorithms include long division or the use of computer code. They require a human to drive them or to set them up.

Let us now delve further back along the chain of creation. We have tentatively identified a faculty to access what is believed to be a God within the minds of believers, and a code enabling this within human DNA, implanted by a supposed creator God through natural selection. The next question is: from where did this algorithm for natural selection come? The short answer is that it is part of a series of natural algorithms, which constitute a teleology driving the evolution of the universe and life. By way of definition a teleology is the doctrine of final causes. It is the view that developments are due to the purpose or design which is served by them. The Theist, if he has followed us thus far, would say the teleology has come from the creator God. He would have created it, along with the laws of science, as a whole series of natural algorithms steering evolution of the universe from the Big Bang to the human brain. What these algorithms would have done is to gradually create complexity and order, within our corner of the universe, out of the chaos of the Big Bang. Together, the whole series of natural algorithms constitute a teleology whose final purpose is to create greater complexity. To go one step further, the Theist might agree with Aristotle, the ancient Greek philosopher: that the final purpose in this case would have been to create man. Each member of the series of algorithms which makes up this teleology would be indispensable to the whole process of creating human beings with their advanced brain. The members of the series, which we can call the chain of creation include: the Big Bang; the consequent expansion of the universe consisting of gaseous hydrogen and helium; the conglomeration of these gases into galaxies, and thence into stars; the manufacture of carbon by nuclear fusion at the center of giant stars; the dispersion of this carbon, along with heavy elements throughout the universe by the explosion of these giant stars in supernovae; the aggregation of this cosmic dust around our sun into planets, with one planet at the goldilocks distance that would support life; the origin of first life on earth, possibly out of a primeval soup or at deep-sea volcanic vents; and the evolution of primitive life to intelligent humans. The odds against this series of events leading to human beings, based on the laws of physics alone, are slim indeed, even with the 14 billion year life of the universe to play with. Atheists would claim that the odds are high enough for this to occur naturally somewhere, sometime within the immense universe. That this is so, is evidenced by the fact that we are here to tell this tale. However, the argument I am presenting here is that the natural laws of physics may have needed some help from a series of natural algorithms, yet to be fully discovered, that constitute a teleology whose purpose is to create greater complexity in our part of the universe, culminating in humans with their advanced intelligence.

A Transcendental Truth

If a creator God is responsible for this teleology, then what else needs to be attributed to him? The teleology would be the workhorse which brings the creation about. But, even before that there must have been the theoretical potentialities for the universe. The teleology would then have been able to choose the best way among these potentialities, utilizing the laws of physics. For the potentialities to exist, there must be some kind of theoretical Transcendental Truth, *but for which nothing could be or be conceived to be.* A transcendental truth is one that is presupposed in, and is necessary to, experience. That transcendental truth would include the laws of physics and mathematics, the properties of matter and energy, and the values of the physical constants, along with the teleology. So, where is the supposed creator God in all of this? He must be the possessor of this Transcendental Truth, and he must have set the teleology in motion to begin the creation. To do that he must have caused the Big Bang. He was the First Cause. As Philo of Alexandria argued almost 2 millennia ago, God must have thought up the Logos (the teleology) by which all things are made, and then set it going (with the Big Bang).

A Non-Sentient Creator God

However, for Atheists and those who have their doubts about a sentient creator God, there is another possible explanation that stops short of such a God. Instead of a creator God there could be a non-thinking Transcendental Truth which could exist in its own right as a brute fact. The First Cause could have been the Big Bang, occurring spontaneously as a quantum shift, which would have required no prior cause (Hawking). The new (positive) combination of matter and energy so created would have been offset by the negative energy of gravity created along with it. There are other theories about how the Big Bang came to be, such as that it emerged from a black hole in another universe, or it was born out of a prior universe which collapsed under the force of gravity into a "Big Crunch" (Davies). If either of these be so, there would have been a series of one or more generations of universes before us. But, a quantum shift out of nothing would still have been needed to start off the very first universe in the series.

The teleology, described earlier, could arise from the Transcendental Truth and the Big Bang. This explanation may suit those who believe that it is not logical for a super intelligence to exist prior to the Big Bang. They would argue that it is more logical that intelligence would gradually evolve in the universe as a move towards greater complexity. Whether one opts for this or a creator God is a matter of personal preference, but the end result would be the same, except for concepts of divine intervention, and perhaps immortality and heaven.

The above idea represents a middle ground between the rather Spartan account of the Atheist and the elaborate accounts of the Catholic Church and fundamentalist Christian faiths. It embraces the idea of a faculty enabling access to what is believed to be a God in the mind of the individual, but instead of it being put there by a creator God, this was accomplished by a Transcendental Truth, which made everything possible, and its teleology which steered the evolution of the universe and life, using the laws of physics. These may exist as brute facts, and be all that is necessary for the creation and evolution of the universe and man. In this scheme the creation was not designed by a designer God, but rather was *meant* to be. The teleology does this by choosing the way forward that produces the most complexity, culminating in the human brain; and (hypothetically) places there a faculty for accessing what is believed to be a God in the mind. This is achieved through a code within human DNA put there through natural selection because it had survivability benefits for the individual and his group (and hopefully in the future for humankind). This scheme involves concepts and processes which are not yet fully understood by science. However, it is conceivable that they will one day be understood as natural.

Whatever may be one's personal preference, it is an open question as to whether or not the creation process was fixed from the beginning, i.e. the outcomes were pre-determined, or whether it is a process of exploration to find the best way forward, i.e. non-deterministic. The former is consistent with Newtonian and Einsteinian physics, which apply to the predictable behavior of the heavenly bodies, not to mention the plan of a designer God. The latter is consistent with Quantum Mechanics as applied to sub-atomic particles, which behave in a completely random fashion. The former makes it easier to believe in destiny; the latter in human free will.

You might say that the idea of a Transcendental Truth, its teleology and a faculty for access to what is believed to be a God within the human mind does not form the basis of a religion, but rather of a philosophy. This is because it is largely based on mysteries of the natural, rather than the spiritual, world. These mysteries are still to be unraveled, and to do so will require huge advances in neuroscience and cosmology, among other disciplines. In that sense we are in a similar position to scientific understanding in the 16th C, before gravity, electromagnetism, radioactivity and evolution became known. Since today's unsolved physical mysteries are not spiritual, then you might say that belief in them can hardly be called religious, which usually requires a spiritual basis. On the other hand, let me repeat the words of philosopher William James that: *"religious belief consists of the belief that there is an unseen order, and that our supreme good lies in harmoniously adjusting ourselves thereto"*. The *unseen order* could be embodied in the Transcendental Truth and teleology I have been describing, along with the laws of physics and mathematics. This fits in with James's definition of religion. As to belief in immortality, an essential part of most religions, there is no reason why the Transcendental Truth and its teleology could be any less efficacious than a creator God in granting immortality. It may be "in the stars" or "on the cards", for all we know. We do not yet know how this could be done. One futuristic possibility is that we could be resurrected in digital form in a super-intelligent future – a kind of "heaven". For those interested in this possibility I refer them to my book "God in the Time of the Internet" and to Michio Kaku's book "The Future of the Mind".

The idea of a Transcendental Truth and its teleological process is analogous to God and his Logos, as envisaged by Philo of Alexandria almost 2000 years ago. The Logos was a term coined by the (Greek) Stoic philosophers before it was adopted by Judaism and Christianity. The Stoics referred to the "Logos" as "the divine animating principle pervading the universe". Logos is Greek for "word", although it was understood by philosophers at the time to mean "wisdom" or "reason". Philo adapted it to Jewish theology prior to his death in 50 AD. He maintained that God conceived the Logos, and then put it to work on the universe. The Gospel of John, written just after, identifies the Logos, through which all things are made, as divine, and further identifies Jesus as the incarnate Logos. *"In the beginning was the Word, and the Word was with God, and the Word was God"* (John 1:1).

Bibliography

Allport, Gordon, "The Individual and his Religion", MacMillan, 1950.

Aslan, Reza, "No God but God", Random House, 2011.

Bear, Mark & Connors, Barry, Neuroscience: Exploring the Brain", Lippincott et al, 2015.

De Chardin, Teilhard, "The Phenomenon of Man", Harper Perennial, 1976 (first published 1955).

Darwin, Charles, "The Origin of The Species", Penguin Classics, 2009 (first published 1859).

Davies, Paul, "The Mind of God", Simon & Schuster, 1993.

Dunlap, K. "Religion: its foundation in Human Life", McGraw-Hill, 1946.

Dawkins, Richard, "The God Delusion", Bantem Press, 2006.

Dixon, Franklin Lonzo, "Spinoza's God", Alondra Press, 2010.

Hamer, Dean, "The God Gene: How Faith is Hard-wired into our Genes", Anchor, 2005.

Hardy, Alister, "The Spiritual Nature of Man", Oxford University Press, 1979.

Hawking, Stephen & Mlodinow, Leonard, "The Grand Design", Bantem Press, 2010.

Hood, Ralph, Hill, Peter & Spilka, Bernard, "The Psychology of Religion", Guilford Press, 2009.

Hvidtjorn. D, et al, "Familial Resemblance in Religiousness in a Secular Society: a Twin Study", Twin Res Hum Genet, 2013 Apr; 16(2) 544-53. Epub 2013 Feb.

James, William, "The Varieties of Religious Experience", Modern Library, 2002 (published 1902).

Jeeves, Malcolm & Brown, Warren, Neuroscience, Psychology & Religion", Templeton, 2009.

Kaku, Michio, "The Future of the Mind", Doubleday, 2014.

King James Version, "Holy Bible".

Marcus, Gary, "The Future of the Brain" Princeton University Press, 2015.

McNamara, Patrick, "Where God and Science Meet" Volume 1, Praeger, 2006.

Nagel, Thomas, "Mind & Cosmos", Oxford University Press, 2012.

Neusner, Jacob, "World Religions in America", Wiley, 2009.

Newberg, A., D'Aquili, E. & Rause, V. "Why God Won't Go Away", Ballantine, 2001.

Searle, John, "Mind", Oxford University Press, 2004.

Shirvington, Phillip, "God in the Time of the Internet", Amazon Kindle, 2014.

Smith, Huston, "The World's Religions", HarperCollins, 1991 (first published 1958).

Solomon, Robert & Higgins, Kathleen, "A Short History of Philosophy", Oxford Press, 1996.

Spector, Tim, "What Twins Reveal about the Science of Faith", Popular Science, Aug. 2013.

Tipler, Frank, "The Physics of Immortality", MacMillan, 1995.

Van de Lans, Jan, "Frame of Reference as a Pre-requisite for The Induction of Religious Experience Through meditation: an Experimental Study", in "Advances in Psychology of Religion", P127-134, Brown, L. B., Oxford: Pergamon Press, 1985.

Wade, Nicholas, "The Faith Instinct", Penguin Press, 2009.

Wilson, David Sloan, "Darwin's Cathedral", University of Chicago Press, 2002.

Wright, Robert, "The Evolution of God", Little Brown & Co., 2009

Yunai, Itai & Lercher, Martin, "The Society of Genes", Harvard University Press, 2016.

www.ingramcontent.com/pod-product-compliance
Lightning Source LLC
Chambersburg PA
CBHW051822040426
42447CB00006B/329